Flavor of a Family

through the sentiments of a father

Nelson S.W. Chang

PRINTED IN THE UNITED STATES OF AMERICA

First Edition published 2008

Permission has been granted from:

Dr. Kelly B.T. Chang for the use of her poem, "Little Feet and Little Faces." © 2001 by Dr. Kelly B.T. Chang

Dr. Kelly B.T. Chang, Erin ("Elina") Wells and Tyrone Wells for the use of the lyrics to their song, "Little Feet and Little Faces," © 2006 by Dr. Kelly B.T. Chang, Erin ("Elina") Wells and Tyrone Wells

Erin ("Elina") Wells for the use of the lyrics, to her song, "Hands," © 2003 by Erin ("Elina") Wells

Kevin K.J. Chang, Esq. for the use of his poetic prose

ISBN 978-0-578-01548-4

This book is dedicated to my wife, Carol L. Chang, my children, Kevin K.J. Chang, Esq., Dr. Kelly B.T. Chang and Erin (aka "Elina") Wells, and to Tyrone Wells, my son-in-law, and my mother and father, Alice and Dai Bew Chang, all of whom were the inspiration for this book and the source of my passion for writing it.

Family begins with life and is perpetuated in life. It

succors and comforts unconditionally, and

nourishes and grows love abundantly. It is

the hope for all mankind,

a blessing of our Creator.

Nelson S.W. Chang

Contents

CHAPTER ONE

In the Beginning

East meets West; West wins. Irish Lassie tames Asian boy.

"Every parting was preceded by sighs, expressions of pain, and long, breathless kisses. We would hold our embrace as long as we could as though fighting against the passing of time and dreading the inevitable separation."

In the first week of January 1968, a pretty brown-haired Caucasian girl with hazel eyes fluttered her eyelashes in my ear as we danced to the music. It was at a joint social event arranged by the men of Collier Hall and the women of Robbins Hall at the University of Oregon. Her name was Carol.

She was a dorm counselor at Robbins, and I was a counselor at Collier. The dance was held in the common lounge of two residence halls. I was into the last two quarters of my third and final year of law school; she was completing the last quarter of her undergraduate degree.

Her hair was in pigtails, and she was smiling at me as she sat by the red brick fireplace. She looked at me and held her look for an instant; when I looked back, our eyes caught and she shyly looked away at the floor and shifted her feet back and forth playfully. Then she looked up at me again and smiled. As I approached her, she fixed her look on me and smiled approvingly. She was a pretty Irish lassie with deep dimples, brown hair and rosy cheeks on a flawless complexion. Since we were the leaders in our respective dormitories, we thought that we should encourage the students to dance by leading off the first one. At least that's what I thought we thought. At the time I was not looking for or wanting a relationship, but as we danced she pulled me closer to her and gently placed her cheek up against mine. It seemed that her cheek never parted from mine as we talked, but the feel of her warm breath on my neck, the warmth of her body, her gentleness, softness and good humor and witty conversation sparked my interest. As we danced throughout the evening, and when we said our extended goodbyes in the stairwell to the women's dorms, she repeatedly sent out clear signals, in many feminine and charming ways, that she wanted to get to know me better.

What followed was a whirlwind courtship. It took all of three months before I asked her to marry me. It started with a movie from which we were distracted by the mischief of a darkened theater. We continued that mischief onto the dance floor of the student union, at a roller-skating party at which we were all alone on a crowded rink, and then at a picnic among the sand dunes far from the others. Intimate escapes, naughty interludes, tender expressions, and countless breath-stealing kisses later, we were in love. And by March she had become a sweet obsession.

She was that wondrous distraction that nearly caused me to flunk out of law school in my third year. She was that ever-present sense, like wildflowers in a spring meadow, which lingered in the air, whispering tha every moment without her was a lifetime wasted. There was no room for learning, no abiding exquisite case distinctions and long lectures; my every thought was of her, my every sigh for her. She had drugged me with a delicious potion of beauty and charm, and I was hopelessly lost.

In the midst of campus, we stood and held each other under an umbrella and kissed that lingering kiss that stole our breaths. Her lips and her touch sustained me. As the tides to the moon, every part and all of me moved to her. The cold of the Oregon night blushed at the warmth of our embrace. Raindrops beat, beat, beat above us like a thousand would-be peepers knocking, and frustrated, fell to the ground in exhausted puddles at our feet. People passed nearby like distant shadows whispering in the night. They could not see us. We were invisible. We were insensible to any world outside the circle of our embrace.

The Emerald Isles had reached far across the globe to an island boy of Asian heritage to kindle such a conflagration. Friends – fellow dorm counselors, student housing staff and administrators on this venerable, ivy-covered, red brick college campus -- who knew of it, fanned the flames like enthusiastic co-conspirators. We would have to win over our parents. In love's commitment, we plotted to make it a perpetual flame.

It was as though I watched myself from a distance asking for her hand in marriage even before I could have given such a proposal the serious thought such proposals deserved. I wanted her; I needed her; I was madly in love with her. I found it impossible to breathe without her, and I was not going to be deterred from my purpose by the soberness of thought and duration of reflection that such a grave proposal demanded. I was out of control and desperate to seize the gold ring before it passed.

That spontaneous, arguably irrational act turned out to be one of the very best of my life. It was one of those times, when looking back on a life, one asks, "What disaster would have befallen me if I had not been so foolish?" Now, I find myself in the happy position of asking myself why she married me at all. I knew I was attractive, but was I *that* attractive?

As we pursued our romantic, sweet madness to become each other's for life, we conspired to and planned how we would sell this interracial partnership to our parents. This would have been the first of its kind in her family and the second in mine. In the 1960s, such marriages were still uncommon. Dropping it upon them like a thunderbolt had been ruled out, and so we planned to administer the news of our nuptial intentions in little doses, all to culminate in my asking her father for her hand.

It was in March of 1968 when I was first introduced to Carol's parents as "just a friend." They were on campus that day for her graduation. That was the first dose, but because the first dose had to be small and seemingly innocuous, I did not participate in the day's events. To have done so would have resulted in too much of their attention being paid to this casual friend. She spent most of that day with her parents and family. After they had gone and later that evening, she surprised me, and we celebrated her graduation as only a couple in love could, all alone and in each other's arms.

In June of 1968, my mom and dad and sister arrived in Oregon to witness and celebrate my graduation from law school. This was an opportunity to administer yet another dose. We would introduce our parents to each other. To that end, my family was invited to Carol's home for dessert. Before that time, however, due to many hints culminating in Carol's coaxing from her parents the invitation for dessert, suspicion had already gripped her parents and sister Kathi. Tickled by the notion and goaded by her mischievous disposition, Kathi playfully strived to fuel their parents' growing anxiety by occasionally trumpeting around their house, "Guess who is coming for dessert?"

I was so captivated at that time, so delirious with love, that although I managed a tenuous grip on reality, it was as though I was living a fairy tale. It was a fairy tale turned real, and I was living it. I was on a quest for the hand of the beautiful Princess Carol. She had enchanted me in many ways, including the tear-filled manner in which she would hold my eyes in hers and weave her spell over me when she sang, "Well, I don't know what it is that makes the flowers grow, and I don't know what it is that makes me love you so." In the playfulness of our intimacy, she would amorously call me her "crazy oriental boy" and I would respond with as much affection by calling her my "crazy Caucasian girl", and that is how we would close letters and notes that passed between us. Admittedly, we shared some amusement in the mischief the interracial component of our proposed union presented. There were times when we were thrilled just to hear each other breathing at both ends of a long distance call; even an unfilled second became a pause that was passionate and loving. Every parting was preceded by sighs, expressions of pain, and long, breathless kisses. We would hold our embrace as long as we could as though fighting against the passing of time and dreading the inevitable separation. When we were in an embrace, it seemed as though she were breathing for me, and when we separated it was as though it took a knife cleaver to do it. When she had reached home, she would sometimes call me collect, but ask the operator to speak to some other named person; we would hear each other's voice on the line and I would know that all was well, that she had safely arrived at her destination. I would wait by my phone in my dorm room anticipating the call and anxious to hear her voice again for I had not heard it for an eternity since we parted a few hours ago.

I am even now still living that fairy tale. She still is everything to me. Our marriage has been blissful, and though our life together is not ended, I can truly say after 40 years that we have "lived happily ever after." What prince can boldly claim as much even before the last chapters of the tale are written?

In all of our plotting and scheming, we could not have predicted that we were igniting the chain of events that would launch this book more than 40 years later.

A new family moved into the neighborhood across the street from us. With them was a fine-looking 5-year-old boy who was given to skipping up and down the walkway in front of their house. One day, when I was working in the front yard, this young boy called out to me from across the street. He asked, "Hey, mister. Are you a stranger?" Even before I was able to recover from the humor of what he asked, his next statement threw me into fits of laughter. "I'm not allowed to speak to strangers. So, if you're a stranger, I can't talk to you," he said.

Newly minted parents ignore their own admonition every time they take up the acquaintance of little strangers in maternity wards across the globe. They not only embrace strangers, they take them into their homes, and they fall in love with them. They fall in love with them as soon as they see them. It is love at first sight in its truest sense, yet the source of so much love for strangers remains a mystery.

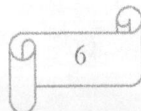

Such spontaneous love seems wildly insane. Taking in and making a lifetime commitment to a naked, friendless, penniless little stranger, who comes with no references, would undoubtedly bring many years of consequences to the lives of the parents and everyone in the household, not the least of which would be a commitment of time, dedication and great financial costs.

When I was an undergraduate and a 24-year-old law student, I don't think I ever thought much about having children someday. Indeed, as a young adult preoccupied with completing my education and adjusting to the world, my experience with children did not endear me to them. I mean, as I grew up seeking direction in life, struggling for high school and college degrees that would attest to my ability to find my way in the world, and coping with my rampant hormones, children that I encountered did not seem cute or adorable. They seemed like bundles of sweaty energy that loudly demanded to distract me from the precious little time I had. I could not talk to them on any sort of intelligent level; they were beyond reasoning with. The word "no" only seemed to energize them into some incomprehensible behavior just as irritating as the one before. Yet, I must have wondered why, when I had been their age, I was so much better mannered than they. Who, I thought, would save the children?

At only 24, I was not that far removed from childhood, yet it seemed that I had no memory of ever being one, nor could I, at that time, have been persuaded that I ever was one. I had no memory of my infancy, of course. I did not remember that first breath that I drew; I did not remember my first or my last diaper; I did not remember ever wetting or soiling one. The idea, of course, was repulsive to me. I did not remember ever being unsteady on my feet. It seemed that I had always walked and talked. And if you asked me then, I would have sworn that I walked out of the womb greeting and thanking the attending physician and nurses in the delivery room, all the while complaining about the bright lights in my eyes.

So, where then was my infancy? As it is for most people, it had been deleted. If you asked us for the date of our birth, we must rely upon the birth certificate and what others, who claim to know, have told us.

So then where was my adolescence? Well, I must admit to having had some memory of those years. Not too much, mind you. I do remember snatches of playing hide-and-seek, war games and sling shot with paper bullets in a narrow lane that seemed wide at the time, and of being raised in a small single-frame, termite-damaged house with a rusting corrugated metal roof that seemed large at the time. I don't recall doing much walking in those days. I ran.

I ran with tattered jeans and bare feet everywhere. I was fast on my feet and could change direction in an instant; I was difficult to catch. That was one reason why other boys sought me out to play on their football team. I never stopped running from the time I awoke until my day ended. I have no memory of sitting. There was too much playing and acting-out to do and too many others my age to get back at; there was too much yelling and screaming to do to awaken the world to the fact that I was here. If it had not been for the adults, I am sure that many of the uncooperative or hostile children in my neighborhood would never have seen the next day.

In those days, the summers seemed long, yet the days were never long enough to finish my games of marbles, football, yoyo, basketball and trading cards. When the sun raced through the sky on a summer day, I bounced the basketball on an outdoor, neighborhood court until I could not see the hoop through the falling darkness. I dragged myself and my basketball home to the reality of brushing my teeth, washing the day's sweat and grime off my body, donning my pajamas and taming the unrestrained enthusiasm for the next day's games when I would soar again.

The next day would be when I would fly over the neighborhood looking down upon and laughing at the other kids below as Superman did when he flew through the sky. There was no telling where I would fly tomorrow. My day ended, but I knew and resented the fact that the world outside my warm blanket and outside the darkness of my little room continued without me. Ending the day beneath the blankets at a reasonable hour in the evening was my greatest dread. What was I missing while I slumbered? What games were played without me? Days would never end if it weren't for those adults who forced it on those who were smaller than they.

I still carry with me scattered mental snapshots of my adolescent and teenage years. Those are the years, I think, that are principally responsible for my alienation from the little people from whose ranks I came. In elementary school, my hips grew faster than the rest of my body and raised concerns in me that I may turn into a girl. The thought, of course, was terrible in my eyes. I would actually tremble at the prospect. I feared that the other boys would not want me on their team if they believed I was a sissy. I imagined taunts, jeers, and all kinds of unwarranted consequences. Those fears, however, quickly changed as my disproportionate growth righted itself and I began to become aware of girls. I could not understand why I was concerned about what they thought of me, but I was. I never wanted to play with them because they were not interested in war games, football and basketball. Their intentional show of disdain for what I thought to be perfectly acceptable behavior -- when I spat into the water fountain or when I threw sand into their faces at the beach -- became an annoyance to me. The girls would huddle together and make a conspicuous display of disapproval, often sneering, snidely whispering, giggling, pointing and showing their backs. It seemed as though girls thought that they were endowed with a unerring talent for knowing what was and was not appropriate behavior. They seemed incapable of understanding my superio motives, and I could not understand why I cared if they cared. I was the beginning of a confusing time in my life as I struggled t understand the puzzling behavior of the opposite sex.

As I began to enjoy social dancing and dating, my mind became even more perplexed as I grew more and more caring about what they were caring or thinking. It would have been a good time for divine intervention. I mean it would have been a suitable time for an angel of God to have told me that there was no understanding them, that even *He* did not understand them, and that to engage in such a futile process was maddening and deleterious to my mental well-being. Well, there was no divine intervention, and I must admit that I was mentally ill for long periods of time. Perhaps, it was this emotional adjustment and the physical awakening in me caused by runaway hormones that purged any memory of my childhood and dimmed my memory of my teenage years, so scorching and so traumatic it was. Perhaps, male maturity comes when men realize the universality of this process, that is, that no man is spared.

Up to and at 24 years of age, I had no room in my life for children. It was not on my wish list to Santa Claus, and I never prayed for the opportunity to become a father. At age 24, I just wanted women. I craved women. The logical, natural, long-term consequence of that desire was not factored in. Nope, I did not think about being a father until it happened. It just happened. It was not planned. I mean having children was planned -- that was not an accident. It was the "becoming a father" part that I hadn't thought about. It is an emotional and spiritual journey. It's a changing, a transformation and a metamorphosis. I did not go to school or take courses to become a father. I did not receive a degree or certificate of recognition for having completed a seminar on the subject. It was not my ambition to become a father. It just fell upon me. I shall tell you how it came to be.

Before little strangers came into our lives, Carol and I enjoyed three wonderful, fun-filled years of starting our lives together and knowing each other. I had alerted the U.S. Air Force that I was married, that I had graduated from law school and that I was licensed to practice law in the state of Hawaii. This would mark the end of my educational deferment from military service during the Vietnam War. We soon got my military orders, and in January of 1969, my beautiful bride and I flew out of Hickam Air Force Base to Omaha where, to my amazement, the trees were bare of leaves and snow was ever present on the ground and the winter cold did not wear well with shorts, aloha shirts or bare feet.

I was forced to accept heavier garments in that harsh Nebraska winter, full of cold feet and hands, scarves and ear muffs, cold feet and hands, frequent difficulties starting our Volkswagen Bug, dark days and frigid winds, tingling ears and more cold feet and hands.

Needless to say, this was all very strange and disconcerting to a boy born and raised in Hawaii. I was used to feeling the warm sand giving way under my feet and squeezing through my toes; I was used to lumpy beach towels under my back, the sound of waves breaking, the fizzling foam and the brushing of sand as the waves reached far up the beaches, the wind blowing through the leaves of coconut and plumeria trees and the smell of sun tan lotion. I was not used to wearing thermal socks that took up any extra room between my feet and my shoes. I was used to sunlight and warm precipitation on my bare face and back; I was not used to freezing precipitation that covered paths with ice and made them treacherous. It seemed that those used to such conditions from years of exposure (including my wife) found great sport and humor in my discomfort.

All we owned at that time were our clothes, some towels and silverware and about $2,000 in cash wedding gifts. We bought our first pieces of furniture: a green sofa bed, a queen-size bed, dressers, dining room set and a rocking chair. We received some used furniture, a recliner, lamps, utensils and end tables from Carol's parents who were downsizing their home. We scrounged around garage sales and thrift shops for other items, more lamps and a wooden ice box we converted into a liquor cabinet. We repainted or re-covered some of them. Carol found discarded old Christmas tree ornaments on a trash heap; we used them for our very first Christmas tree. With all of these we were able to furnish a two-bedroom apartment during my three years of active military service.

During that time, we traveled in a cobalt blue VW (purchased right off of the showroom floor in Council Bluffs, Iowa), adorned in chrome and equipped with a useless air conditioner. It took us away from the Midwest, to the West and East coasts, down to the Mexico, Texas, Louisiana and Mississippi, Georgia and Florida and up to and through Canada, New England, New York and Washington, D.C.

We even toured (without the car) Scotland, England, Holland, France, Germany, Austria, Switzerland and Italy. We met friends at Heathrow Airport and drove up through Scotland, wending our way through misty moors as we battled thoughts of ghosts on the edge of windswept, inky lochs. We drank warm beer in an English pub and found much fun in struggling to comprehend the cockney accent. We dropped in at a London courthouse to get out of the rain, and we poked fun at the wig-bedecked barristers with long black sideburns that mocked the archaic custom. Hand in hand, we scoured the architecturally fascinating twists and turns, colonnades, cornices, squares, bridges and channels of the City of Venice, marveled at Venetian glass blowing, loved the romance of it all and regretted that our stay in Venice was so brief. Amidst the press of tourists, I fell asleep on the floor of the Sistine Chapel while on my back marveling at Michelangelo's ceiling fresco of the Creation. Carol climbed the Tower of Pisa and drove the Italian men mad in her leather miniskirt. We dined in Paris along the Seine, and when asked "Avez-vous reservation?" we offended the waiter by responding in a culturally tactless confusion of English. We ambled down the Champs Elysee, ascended the Arch de Triomphe and took the wrong turn up and down the Eiffel Tower. Carol was flashed at the Roman Coliseum, but later complained that the poor lighting kept her from getting a good view of the goods on display. If only she'd been paying more attention! We enjoyed fondue in Switzerland and climbed onto huge beer kegs and drank from large carafes of beer in Germany, and we burned votive candles in magnificent cathedrals.

Instead of *her* friends and *my* friends, we began new relationships with *our* friends. We began building *our* lives together, *our own* experiences, *our own* traditions and *our own* memories. She became my constant companion, my best friend and confidant and my lover. Two lives were becoming one, and traces of our past lives as singles began to fade.

In the last part of the third year of military service, Carol just announced that it was time; she was going off the pill. She took the lead. There was no argument, no debate and no extended discussion. I assented. That was that. It was that simple. She led. I followed. I am glad she did and I am glad I followed, for from that tacit assent came forth so much to speak of here. I had no idea what a ride I was in for.

I was madly in love with my wife, and the notion of having more of her through children just seemed another exciting way to complete our love. I liked the idea of reproducing ourselves. Multiplying ourselves was to me like multiplying our love. Since loved to love her, I wanted more of her. I was fascinated with the idea that the passion between us could create more of us. We were curious about what we could brew and how they would look, particularly since I was Chinese and she was an assortment of Irish, Welsh and German.

Parks would be just pieces of abandoned land if they were not cluttered with screaming kids. Swings, seesaws and climbing structures would be but silent curiosities if there were no clambering little urchins. We would all be the poorer if we did not have to spoon pureed food into toothless mouths and wipe spills off the high chair, table, floor and ourselves, and squander quiet time filling their nimble minds with fairy tales and the Cat in the Hat. Without them there would be no need for fairy tales, Santa Claus, the Easter bunny, Little League, Brownies, Cub Scout camps and picnics, Boy Scouts and playgrounds.

Perhaps, we would be happier not having to deal with the fuss of Christmas, Easter, Halloween and other such seasonal events enjoyed mostly by children. Colored lights, plastic trucks and little socks and shoes would no longer clutter our living rooms; everything would be in its place, and we would not have to be distracted from our favorite TV programs or even take tim from important business for warm hugs and sloppy wet kisses. Our shoes would not be scuffed and our suit pants ruffled in the morning before work by children clambering to a higher elevation to receive a kiss and a reassuring embrace.

It is too horrible to imagine a world, a neighborhood or a community without children.

CHAPTER TWO

Then Strangers Came

Angel in my bed brings heaven to our house.

A mayonnaise jar full of urine was our first hint that new life was stirring. We were visiting a good friend in California, a gynecologist who gladly took Carol's sample in for testing in Los Angeles. We were on our way back to our civilian lives in Hawaii, and now we would have good news to take back to my mom and dad and family there.

So, we took three strangers into our home, and we named them Kevin, Kelly and Erin. Besides taking my last name, they were given Chinese middle names. My maternal grandfather did the honors of choosing the Chinese middle names for each of them. Our first born's Chinese middle name meant a great man who unites different worlds. Kelly and Erin were given names meaning precious goddess and precious lotus, respectively. Each middle name given to each of them has proven to be prophetic, particularly, the name given to Kevin. We gave them Irish first names because Carol is almost half Irish. Carol and I loved, supported and raised them. We made them and we take full responsibility for what we have done.

As I write this book, we are now empty nesters, so I am able to speak from experience. We have taken strangers into our house, nurtured and loved them and provided for all their worldly needs, food, clothing and shelter, and most of their education. That is my only qualification on this subject. I am just one of many fathers who do the same.

This is just one father's love story, a sentimental rant, told ramblingly through excerpts of some writings, letters and emails written over time and passed within our family. There is a reason why this story of family is "through the sentiments of a father." Sentiments mean feelings. Right or wrong, true or false, sentiments are exclusively owned by the person with the sentiments; thus, there can be no disagreement, quarrel or dispute. It is by design that this writing is short on facts and long on sentiment.

"Flavor of a Family" signifies that this is but a taste of our family. This is not meant to be a diary or a biography, nor is it meant to be an historical or factual portrait of our family. It is not intended to be thorough or complete. This is merely an awkward rewrite of what has come to be written in the heart of a father.

For about six months I'd had a pet love bird I named Sneaks. One day Sneaks refused to come out of his cage. He would snap fiercely at me every time I tried to remove him. He sat at the bottom of his cage for hours picking at old newspaper and rolling the pieces through his beak; it was reminiscent of how people used to roll their own cigarettes from loose tobacco in a pouch and small squares of white paper. This behavior went on for weeks while he would sit in the corner and at the bottom of the cage. I felt hurt that he did not want to come out to play with me. I was used to my pet bird sitting on my shoulder and going wherever I went around the house. I could not understand. I told Carol about it and she went into the next room to observe the bird. When she returned, she asked, "Is that an egg in its cage?" Surprised, I went to see for myself. Indeed, it was! An unfertilized egg. My bird was not a male; she was a female trying to become a mother. She was the female bird that I had ever had. Sneaks had been trying to make a nest out of what little materials she could scrounge up in her cage, and she had been protective of the egg within her. I removed the egg she laid, but she laid another. I removed that egg also, but for weeks after, she continued to lay eggs and refused to come out and play despite all my attempts to coax her out.

Sneaks exhibited a maternal instinct that was just a hint of the maternal instinct that had been so strong within Carol. It was that maternal instinct that made her take the lead in the birth and the raising of our children. This bird was a reminder that having and raising children is really part of who we are. We have come to think of children as an option, an election, a choice of lifestyle rather than life's direction. Today, we have greater control over whether to have children, and maybe that power to influence conception has caused us to forget that, for most couples capable of having children, it is Nature's way. We have come to look at Nature as a third person, unfortunately, an entity separate from ourselves, something we are not a part of.

That maternal instinct was to me like a celestial light that seemed to settle upon Carol before and during her pregnancy. As her husband, it was my blessing to bask in her glow and to be amazed by it. She seemed transformed. Sometimes, it even seemed as though she had been transported to a very warm and delicious place, a very happy place, a place where a husband and father could not go. She seemed infused with a grace, inexhaustible energy and a glow that shone through her and her every movement. It filled the room she was in and touched all that watched her. The growing life within her seemed to have made her even more beautiful than when I first married her. She seemed charged with the purposefulness of the new life within her. It seemed that during motherhood a woman is enabled to love and to rejoice in love beyond earthly limitations.

Even before they came, she had fallen in love with our children, for as they grew within her it was evident that so too did her love for them grow. As the life moved and stirred within her, so too did her excitement and joy soar at their approaching arrival. It seemed that each pregnancy was a dance of love between the mother and the child growing in her, but only they could hear the music.

A father has the privilege of watching the mother with their child dance as though floating on air. Even though the child represented the best of both parents, while growing within their mother, they were as one with her like no husband or father could be. This ever-growing love appeared to imbue her with the stamina and strength of many men. It is the privilege of motherhood that a father could be envious of.

Yet, a father will have his many opportunities to grow close to his children. I did when I danced the endless, memorable dance with my little Kelly who wore a cute yellow dress with the hem slightly above her little knees.

She wore a yellow dress and stood a little more than two lovely feet from the ground. Her brown curly hair fell to her shoulders and she had a matching yellow ribbon in it. She had the cutest, prettiest face in the entire room, and upon that face she wore a prettier smile. Her little hands seemed always to be seeking her mother's, and when they were not, her arms were upraised entreating a hug. Whenever her little arms encircled my neck, I was captive in her charm. She was pure love.

With her arms raised above her shoulders and her hands over her head, her little feet moved to the rhythm of the band even before the festivities began. She was all by herself on the floor swaying to the music. I was amazed that such a new little person knew to move like that in sync with the music of the band. Seeing her up there, I was filled with pride. I was drawn to her. I could not resist. I lifted her in my arms. Her feet were not touching the ground, nor were mine. She put her cheek against mine and held me tightly around my neck. She whispered in her soft little girlish voice, "I love you, Daddy." We seemed frozen in that position. We danced all night. I was conscious of everyone's eyes on us, but I didn't care. I was so proud. She was my little girl. For that moment in time, she was all mine and she was all I cared about.

Mothers know their children long before the fathers lay eyes on them. The child growing within the mother for nine months is, throughout, in intimate communion with the mother in ways that can only be imagined. Nature could not have devised a more ingenious way to introduce a mother to the coming of a child and to prepare both of them for the mutual undertaking and challenges ahead. They share each other's blood, body, thoughts, heartbeat and breath. For during that time they are one in everything and separate in nothing. For that time they share one life, both inseparable and each a part of the other. The child becomes the one that husband and wife had vowed to become; the child is the fulfillment of their matrimonial vows, to cling to each other and to become one flesh. A thousand miracles occur between mother and child that can only be gleaned with awe from observing the mother. It is all reflected in the blossoming beauty of motherhood that a father is blessed to watch up close and personal. So, by the time the child is born, he or she, in actuality, is no stranger to the mother.

Carol seemed to know when she was needed without even a whimper from the newborn. At all hours of the night, she was up and out of bed in a flash. If they even turned in their sleep, she would seem to be aware. Her thoughts were never far from her children. She labored to see to their comfort, to their nourishment, their education and their health. She did it at all times of the day and night without complaint and always, always with grace. She cared for them with love and loved to care for them. To her, raising our children was not just rewarding, it was great fun. Carol loved being a mother to our children.

If angels existed, I imagine that they would be very much like my wife was when she was with child and when she was caring for them. I felt as though I was sleeping with an angel, a person full to the brim with the soft glow of love and caring. It was a husband's privilege to observe this, to be so close to it, and I fell more deeply in love with the angel that she had become.

Angel in the House

Could there be an angel in the house?
I do not believe in angels, but

*In the middle of the night she bounds out of bed as quiet
as a mouse.*

*In every breath she takes, there is happiness and grace.
I do not believe in angels, yet
Behold the depth of care and kindness in her face.*

*There is so much love about her, so much tenderness
and care.
I do not believe in angels, but
There is a joyful twinkle in her eyes and a halo in her
hair.*

*She floats about the crib and room as though on angel
wings.
I do not believe in angels, though
She sings and hums a tune to every little thing.*

*As she nurtures, she sings; there is music in her head.
I do not believe in angels, but
If there be an angel, she is sleeping in my bed.*

Long after my children were grown and out of the house,
I was reminded of the joy of children when I was invited to a
lunch with friends of Erin at a restaurant called Buca di Beppo.
Among her friends were two young mothers armed with infants
whom they brandished with glowing smiles and bubbling pride.
As they talked with friends around the table, they cradled their
infants close as though they were just an extension of their
arms. Occasionally, they would put them over their shoulders
and pat their backs, gently rubbing them reassuringly. They
rocked them and bounced them on their laps, intermittently
kissed them, hugged them, pressed their cheeks to theirs, blew
on their eyelashes, whispered nonsense in their ears, blew
loudly into their tummies, tickled them and smiled into their little

faces. They spoke a lot of gibberish to them as though they were being understood. A bystander could not possibly understand what was being said, yet everyone understood what was being communicated. It was a whole new language that had no meaning except to coax and cajole a reaction from the infant and to exchange affection. Any kind of reaction, a smile, a look of befuddlement, a laugh and even a whimper was received with joy and laughter.

The action was not one way. The infants were smiling back, big smiles, and widening and narrowing their eyes, making faces and pumping their limbs with obvious pleasure and joy. They explored the faces of their mothers with big, curious eyes, and occasionally they would seem to stop at a part of their faces as though riveted by something that struck their fancy. They reached out and touched their mothers' faces with their little hands, sometimes getting their little digits into their mothers' mouths and noses. At times they drew back and started waving their hands and legs gleefully as though they had again discovered something of great interest in their mothers' faces. It was as though they exulted in finally seeing the faces of the women who had been their world for nine months. It was much like watching a conversation between people who did not speak the same language using all their wiles to communicate by gestures, facial expressions, touching , imitating and mimicking, but it was all done with warmth and tenderness and genuine joy.

What was intriguing is that despite all of these tender distractions, the two mothers seemed quite capable of keeping up with the adult conversation around the table. Technological multi-tasking is nothing compared to the skills these mothers seemed capable of. Mothers multitasked long before the word computer became a household word.

Then there came a time when these infants began to whimper. Almost synchronously, without a word to each other or to anyone else, and as though on cue, the mothers covered their upper bodies and their infants with blankets and began to breast feed them in the midst of all their friends and the multitude of customers. Occasionally, seemingly without forethought, they gently patted and rubbed the moving bundles beneath the blankets. All of this unfolded so casually without a break in the conversation. For a person like me who had been deprived of such sights for so long, it was remarkable. It was as though someone turned the lights on in a dark room and no one seemed to notice, no one except me.

Seeing those two young mothers sitting side by side across the table stirred emotions and memories of the time I was blessed with my children and the privilege of watching Carol luxuriating in the blessings of motherhood.

In the middle of so many people, most of whom were other customers sitting at other tables, these mothers continued to tend to their little charges with so much love and warmth, and all this was occurring without notice by most people in the room. In the din of all the idle chatter, pounding of feet, dragging and shuffling of chairs, clinking of forks and knives and scraping on plates, amidst the unknowing customers, the scene of these two mothers with infants seemed to generate all the warmth and energy and pleasantness of a crackling, blazing fire in a large open hearth in a high mountain cabin.

There was an explosion of human tenderness, kindness, life and love, all concentrated in the two chairs these young mothers occupied. I thought to myself that such a moment should not be saved just for the younger generation. There was too much warmth and energy there not to be shared with all the generations of the world. Perhaps, it is for too many of us our greatest misfortune that we have allowed the pleasure and beauty of such moments to become commonplace. Maybe, it is because there is simply too much noise in the world around us.

The role of a father in the raising of children is made invisible by the dazzling halo of a mother's love. It is the lot of fathers to be the stage hand laboring behind the curtains and out of the light.

As my son's graduation from high school approached, I wrote a letter to him.

Dear Son,

Wasn't it just yesterday that we first met? If not, why then are my memories of you unchanged although you have changed? Between now and then my memories seem so distant, so vague, and so cloudy. Yet my memories of you wrapped securely in a blue blanket moments after your first breath are as thrilling to me now as the anticipation of your approaching graduation. As I did then, I swell with pride when I think of you now.

I wonder what good we've done that you have so much more promise than I ever had. I am so excited about what's ahead of you that I want to share every moment, although that can never be. For now, as you move into adulthood, your steps will be your own and without me. I'll be there to catch you if you should stumble, but otherwise you must take the trail by yourself.

A father's life is like running a relay. For awhile we run together, but too soon the time comes when I begin to feel your grasp of the baton tighten, and the other end slipping from my hand; I panic as you kick away; then there is sorrow and sadness as you spurt down the track; sadness will eventually be replaced by joy as I see your speed and exhilaration soar with the roar of the crowd.

I am proud and grateful that I can call you son.

Congratulations, son.

Your Father

Years later, during that season when high schools conducted graduation ceremonies all across the country, I sent that letter in to the editor of our local newspaper. I thought that, maybe, it would speak for a lot of fathers during this time. After was published, I received a call from a father who thanked me for having captured in words so much of his feelings.

There are, perhaps, many fathers who find it very difficult to openly express their feelings about family. Fathers often stand in silence together on the sidelines at football and soccer games and sit without notice in the galleries at speech contests and school plays. Although we may never have met or even spoken to each other, we communed in muted pride, a pride that only fathers seem able to share. It is a pride that seems to want to burst out of our skin, jump out of our hearts and make us scream from the mountain tops. It is a pride that challenges the strongest of us to hold within, yet often fathers suffer to love in the loneliness of that silence.

If you look real hard you will see it. It is in the strain of concealing the unseemly tears welling up in our eyes. It is in the manner we turn away to seek a more private place where our faces will not reveal our feelings. It is in the way we stutter or clear out throats during the applause. It is in the manner with which we resist a gloating, prideful smile, struggle for words and uneasily mutter gratitude when patted on the back for what our children do. It is in our unblinking gaze at a child's performance and in our occasional furtive glances at the faces of others appreciating that performance. It is even in our stony, killer stares at those un-appreciating watchers. You will find it in the shuffling of our feet as we stand nearby, in our fidgeting in the proximity but behind the admirers, in the watching and straining to hear the praises of others. It may be discovered in that brief stolen glance at mother and child even in the midst of an intense conversation with good friends in a busy restaurant. It may be noted in the behavior of a father when he hammers a nail into the house, climbs the ladder to paint it, labors hours into the night, speaks long hours with financial advisors, searches for a suitable insurance policy, and prepares his last will and testament.

We tend to be less vocal than mothers about our feelings. Maybe it's because speaking up about children and family is not considered the manly thing to do. In our culture, it may be looked upon as unbecoming for a man to express so much feeling. Fathers are expected to talk about cars, football, tools and hardware stores. It may be because of a father's belief about how to raise and discipline children; a father must maintain some remoteness to deter bad behavior. Expressions of love expose vulnerabilities. Silence in situations when emotion is usually expected is looked upon as evidence of stoicism, and stoicism equates with strength. The father has been and must remain the hunter, provider and protector. This natural and traditional role is responsible for expectations in members of the family. These expectations generate feelings of comfort and security in other family members. Fathers seem aware that exposing vulnerabilities generate insecurities in those they are responsible for protecting. It may simply be because it is nature's way that men should vent emotions in positive action rather than in verbal expression; flight and avoidance of danger demands quick action.

The free and open expression of love, compassion and kindness are most essential to the actual nurture and raising of children, and women are naturally better equipped to do it. Their voices are sweeter and softer, more suitable for soothing hurts and comforting fears. They are more sensitive. They are gentle and tender in their manner. They are gifted with a delicacy of approach, a kindness and sweetness and empathy for others. Mothers are the softener in the rough and tumble of life. They kiss away the hurt. They make gentler the transition between infancy and adulthood. They smooth the rough edges of a difficult and dangerous world. They are the arbiters between the testosterone-driven protectors of the family and the tender minds and hearts of children. They are "the sugar that helps the medicine go down." None of these traits would befit the defender and protector of the family.

I did not want to be victim of the solitude such cultural and traditional silence inflict. I did not want my children to be victims of it either. I made it a point to always tell my children that I loved them. I would do it at every opportunity, every morning I saw them, every time I left and returned to them, every time I put them to bed or closed a letter.

One night as I put Erin to bed, she asked, "Daddy, why do you always tell me you love me?"

I responded that, "I do it because I have a need to, because it makes me feel good. I do it because I want you to know that I love you and because I never want you to forget. I do it because I never want to fall out of the habit of saying it. I do it because I do love you. I do it because I want you to learn to say it freely."

I am third-generation Chinese American. I was raised in a little, garage-less, termite-eaten, single-frame house owned by my maternal grandparents, built on a small substandard lot. It had rusting corrugated steel roofing that would rumble like the hooves of cattle whenever it was rained on. It was situated off of a narrow lane in a multi-ethnic neighborhood. The milkman, the mail man and the "slop man" had to walk into and through the lane from the street in order to service the houses. It was much less than one-half the size of the house I currently live in. The floors were of old, worn, broken and discolored linoleum. The floor of the kitchen noticeably sloped to one side. The tub and shower stall were of metal and they were old and rusting, but functional and adequate. It was not uncommon to find rat and termite droppings inside, particularly in the dank basement where my grandmother saved remnants of cloth and material in large tied bundles. During heavy rains, we would rush to the basement armed with rags and sponges and buckets to bail the water that poured through the concrete block walls below grade. Almost every other house in our neighborhood was similarly constructed and in similar condition. We lived in a community of immigrants in the city of Honolulu, Territory of Oahu. It was here that I was born and raised; it was here that by virtue of my birth I was fortunate to become an American citizen.

This was a house that provided all I needed. For the most part it was warm, dry and comfortable. It protected me from the weather, gave me privacy and kept me secure. In that house, I never wanted for anything. In those humble surroundings, I was happy and loved.

My parents were blue collar, hard-working and loving people who married just after high school. It seems that they were always struggling to save and make ends meet. The families that lived in that little house saved every cent they made and appreciated every cent they managed to save. I worked as a newspaper boy at Hickam Air Force Base selling papers for 15 cents each; from that, I kept a nickel. My pockets were bulging with loose change. Every penny, nickel or dime I received, I kept in gallon glass jars on a shelf in my room. When I asked for and received a shoeshine box as a gift, I would shine shoes to make extra income. I remember one evening, when I was lying on the bottom bed of a bunk bed that my brother and I shared, my mother stole through the darkness of my little bedroom, sat on my bed beside me, whispered that they needed more money, and quietly pleaded with me to borrow the coins I had saved in my gallon jars. In those days a dime was enough to get us into the movies, but in those days, a dime was difficult to come by.

At any one time that little house was the residence of three or more generations, yet since we were all fam.ily, it never seemed crowded or small. My mother had five other siblings, three sisters and two brothers. They were hard working, generous and loving people. There was something about our family that wherever we were, we could never be crowded. We could never be a crowd.

My maternal grandmother preserved all the fruits we received from friends and neighbors or picked from trees in our neighborhood. Star fruit, mango, lemon, dragon eyes and other fruits were spread out and dried under the sun on a sloping, rusting roof, and later salted and bottled in sweet sour sauce. She would raise, kill, pluck, prepare and cook chicken kept in coops in the back of the house. She spent most of her time laboring over huge pots boiling and steaming all day over a gas stove and over a little makeshift open fire in the back of the house.

I remember how she would use me to help pound rice into flour. I would stand at one end of long heavy board balanced on a metal fulcrum anchored in concrete; at the other end was a heavy cylindrical pistil molded from solid metal that would rise when I pushed down on the other end of the board with my foot, and it would fall of its own weight onto the rice below in a cone shaped hole that had been formed in solid concrete. My grandmother would sweep up the flour and sift it. The grains that were not sufficiently crushed into powder would be put back into the cone shaped hole. The powder was mixed with water until it reached a doughy consistency. Then she kneaded it into little white thin squares, put a variety of meats or sweets inside, and folded them into dumplings and other Chinese delectables.

My maternal grandfather was a scholar who emigrated from China. He was an expert on the abacus. I used to watch in amazement as his fingers flew swiftly over the beads, but I never understood what he was doing; I enjoyed listening to the clicking of the beads. Using a long brush and black ink he rubbed out from a hard ebony-like plate, he hand-wrote beautiful Chinese characters into a long book or onto translucent paper. As a child, I watched him do this, but without any understanding. He had reportedly made a lot of money in business, but lost everything when he signed a note to help a friend. He was known and admired in the community for his education and fine Chinese cooking skills. He spent most of his free days shopping in Chinatown for special spices, dried mushrooms, white and black fungus, fresh seafood and exotic ingredients, and then he would return home to bend over large woks with long spatulas in his hands. He was proud that his family never went hungry, and he toiled to make sure that the shelves in the kitchen and cupboards were always brimming with canned and dry food. Whenever a can was removed, he would quickly replace it so that his family would never see an empty space on the shelf. I cannot remember a day when I went without a meal.

Almost every day, from early morning to night, I heard the banging and clashing of woks, pots and pans and utensils. I could hear the sounds of washing, the sizzle of oil on a hot fire and the washing of dishes, and I could smell the ginger, garlic and spices as they hit the hot pan. Over these sounds and smells I could hear my grandparents speaking in Chinese, a language I could not understand. Sometimes, I could not hear any kitchen sounds over the continuous blaring of Chinese music from the radio. (As a generation born in the United States, my ears were not accustomed to Eastern music. To me, Chinese music was no different from the screeching of tires and the sounds of pile drivers at an urban construction site. Since I was just a kid, my grandparents never asked for my opinion. It was a challenge trying to study at home.) It seemed that from morning to night my grandparents labored arduously to prepare meals for the family.

One thing that was always said in my family was to appreciate and eat everything put before us. When a guest or friend came over, the very first thing my grandparents would ask in Chinese was whether they had eaten yet. And if they hadn't, they would offer the visitors something to eat. It was a custom in traditional Chinese families. This custom likely grew from the scarcity of food in the old country where famine was not uncommon. It was oft repeated by family and friends and driven home by my parents again and again that we were lucky to live in the United States.

The children that lived in our community were Chinese, Portuguese, Japanese, Hawaiian, Caucasian, Okinawan, Korean, Polynesian, Filipino and multi-ethnic mixtures. I knew of no other world except one where everyone was ethnically different. I went to classes with them, ate with them, became acquainted with their culture and cuisine, worked with them, laughed and played with them, and loved and befriended them. Whenever I played with a different friend, I would be exposed to a different culture. When I visited their homes, I ate their food and heard their music streaming from the radio. One evening I'd be enchanted with a blue eyed Polynesian girl dancing the hula at a luau; the next evening, I may be sweating under the lion head or tail in the lion dance at a Chinese New Year celebration while trying to avoid the fire crackers exploding around me and at my feet; in yet another evening, I may be dancing around in a circle at a Bonn dance trying to catch the eyes of pretty Japanese girls in colorful kimonos at a Buddhist temple. The next day, I may find myself walking a cute Okinawan girl home from school or complaining about the loud music from the Chinese opera at a theater nearby. It was the blessing of daily life in Hawaii that I became accustomed to living in a community where race, culture and language were richly diverse and that diversity a daily part of our lives; for those so blessed, we had become the children of diversity; diversity had become a part of who we were. If I fought with anyone, it was never because of any racial differences; it was simply because they were wrong and I was right. It was my basketball and I made the rules.

We walked together in bare feet to elementary school. I seldom ever wore any footwear. I remember that when the pavement was too hot, I would dance around very quickly, moving from one shaded spot to the next, jumping like a worm in a bean, and if there were no shaded spots, I would walk on the grassy areas or run as though the wake from my speed would cool the soles of my feet. My feet were tough in those days, and I could play for hours on the pavement of an outdoor basketball court without suffering for it the next day. Sometime before I moved on to intermediate school, the teachers began insisting that we wear shoes or slippers. It soon became a school requirement. I recall how much I rebelled against the idea of wearing anything on my feet. I thought, at that time, that it was torture to confine and suffocate feet with leather or rubber. (My disposition was such that I found myself very sympathetic to horses that were shoed with nails and the hammer of a blacksmith.) It was an unjust encroachment on my personal comfort. I was perfectly happy as a shoeless Hawaiian street urchin and as an unruly free spirit (Or, if you will, "pest.") of my neighborhood.

As I was growing up, it was my observation that first- and early-generation immigrant parents seemed to have difficulty expressing themselves; communication was difficult. Perhaps, it was in part because, for many, English was not their first language, and because, when English was attempted, understanding was afflicted by the inflections of the many different tongues spoken in our community. Moreover, their children were being schooled in the language of their adopted country, and so English had become their children's first language. My maternal grandfather spoke almost no English, and my maternal grandmother spoke very little English. Their friends were mostly of their generation from the old country and so they spoke their native tongue to each other. My father did not want me to go to Chinese language school, saying that it was more important to my success to learn and master English, the language of the United States.

So, other than for a few words and broken phrases in Chinese, I could not speak to my grandparents when I was growing up. Although they tried to teach me, it never took. They talked to me, praised, scolded or instructed me in Chinese, and so I never did understand much of what was said by them except through gleaning some meaning from their faces and manner. I don't have a memory of them ever telling me they loved me or even of my ever telling them that I loved them. Yet, from their behavior, I came to know that they loved me. When I grew older I realized what a terrible loss it was to me. The barriers of culture and language coupled with the incapacity of childhood had stolen a treasure of knowledge, wisdom and love that was right in my lap. It was there near me, right in front of me, and I did not have the vision to see it nor the maturity of heart and mind to know it. What other precious things, I wonder, escaped my discerning because of that incapacity?

While the earlier-generations of immigrants pushed their children to get a good education, to learn to speak and write English well and to succeed in their new country, they must have sensed that by doing so they were building a wall of silence around themselves. With each successive generation the wall grew higher and higher as less and less Chinese was spoken. My grandparents were often and increasingly left out of familial conversations at our many dinners and parties. While children naturally pull away from their parents and grandparents as they pursue their own lives, there is no doubt but that we were increasingly estranged from our grandparents, and to a lesser extent from our parents, by reasons of culture, language and education. It must have been very painful for them. It was a sacrifice that they quietly made, for they knew it to be essential to the success and happiness of their children, grandchildren and great grandchildren. They quietly suffered the wall to continue to grow around them. As I grew up, I could not communicate with my grandparents. I did not know it then, but their sufferance of this wall of silence was an act of love. I wish I had had the understanding then to know that I was loved so very much. Maybe, for some of us, our difficulties in life are not that we are not loved, but that we don't know that we are loved.

I also think that the culture in immigrant families required that the father be the strong figure. In our traditional Chinese family my grandfather was always held with respect and reverence. When I lived with them there was never a question of who was in charge. My grandfather and father were. Authority and discipline fell to fathers. Expressions of pain and emotions were viewed as signs of weakness. Perhaps, this was necessary in the old country where life was more intense and conditions for life more severe, survival more difficult. For survival of the family a strong figure was absolutely necessary, someone to be in command, someone with physical strength to lead the family out of danger, someone who had the physical strength to engage in the hard labor required to earn the food to sustain the family. In times of danger, the family had to respond to a father's commands in a disciplined manner. Perhaps, in today's world in this great country -- one of comfort, abundance and security -- the role of a man has been changing, roles are confused. Maybe that is why some men may feel lost.

I saw how difficult communication between the different generations was. I sensed how difficult it was between fathers and mothers, aunties and uncles and cousins and even friends. I observed how difficult it was for many families in the multi-ethnic, multi-lingual, multi-cultural community I grew up in. I witnessed how an inability to express oneself, one's thoughts and feelings confined a person to loneliness and frustration. My grandparents and I were separated by a language and a culture that robbed us of the intimacy we should have had. I also observed how the lack of good communication led to so much misunderstanding, mischief and heartbreak. I did not want that for myself, and I certainly did not want it for my family. In part, this is why I earned my undergraduate degree in English, why I excelled in languages, received so many awards in Latin and why I went on to law school. I concluded that misunderstanding due to language and culture was the biggest factor causing a breakdown in relationships, anger, frustration and disagreements. As a boy, I used to read about and admire great orators and advocates. I wanted to become an advocate for those who were unable to be an advocate for themselves.

Here and now, I sum up the message of this writing as boldly and succinctly as I can. I say what many fathers likely feel but do not often say. Marrying my wife and raising and loving children have been rewarding and satisfying. It has been the greatest challenge of my life. It has been happy, loving and fulfilling. Marrying my wife and accepting these strangers into my life have been the very best decisions of my life. Through the love of family I built a world of contentment to shelter me from the real world of many challenges and problems. Now, as I have grown wiser, I know more keenly than I ever did before that my family was and is my life. My true mission in life was not to become an attorney and to practice law. It was to become a husband and a father. My career and my work existed to serve my family, never the other way around. Many of us know this, but do not remember.

What we see is not necessarily what we perceive. How we react to and how we feel about what we see seem to arise more from perception than from what is actually seen. We perceive others differently if they are longtime friends rather than mere acquaintances, and we act toward them accordingly. Our behavior toward women changes when we are physically attracted to them. How we perceive what we see is bent by our feelings at the time. Although we may see the same things, we do not perceive them the same way. When we are with those we love, staring into the star-filled firmament may be an event more memorable than when we are with those with whom we feel indifferent. When we are alone on a windy hill, staring into that same sky may fill us with sadness or melancholy. A walk in the busy streets of a large city is different when we are alone than when we are in the same city arm in arm with the love of our life.

Children too are perceived differently, such as when they are pesky little siblings who come down the stairs to see who is dating their big sister, as opposed to our very own children who are the creation of our love. Just as the woman I fell in love with did, children of my own blessed me with a different perspective on the world and on life. They enabled me to see the world and my life through different eyes. The creativity of an artist is enabled by his ability to capture on canvas, in a song or in gnarly piece of driftwood, more what he perceives than what he sees. It may be difficult for some to appreciate the joy of having their own children unless they are enabled as parents to see through the powerful and colorful prisms of parenthood.

Without children we would not have to bother with inane little questions like, "Mister, are you a stranger?", "Why don't clouds fall down?" or "What are in the spaces between the black stripes of a zebra?" or "Who painted the spots on a leopard?", or even "Why do our butts eat up the bottom of our panties?"

Without little strangers we would not have childish chatter that makes us laugh and titillates our creative side, the part of our brain that once told us all dreams were possible. Fairy tales and fantasies are for those young, trusting minds not hemmed in by life's experiences. Fairy tales and fantasies are not frequently visited by adults, that is, not until a little stranger enters their lives. Little strangers come with free tickets to fantasies and fairy tales and these tickets allow them to be accompanied by their adult parents.

Infants make us laugh. They are not like stand-up comedians; they do not have pre-canned jokes and one-liners. Their expressions reveal feelings, honest and undisguised. They make us laugh just by a smile or by enigmatic expressions as if to say: "Who are you, and why are you in my pants?"; "Is this a bath? Help! I just peed all over myself."; "I just met you; why are you talking like a baby?"; "What did you say? Huh, what did you say?"; "I don't know who I am. I don't know why I'm here. Please inform the authorities where I am."; "Don't touch me there. Don't."; "This high chair is just so uncomfortable."; "What is this yuk you are putting into my mouth? I want the boob."; or "It wasn't me. Who cut that one?"

Watching an infant have a BM in his diaper illustrates this. We are fortunate that we are not usually privy to the expressions on adult faces when they have a BM. In a modern, civilized world it is one of those blessings from which we have been spared. It would not be a pretty sight, nor, I am sure, would it bring much amusement. In contrast, watching an infant in the throes of producing one in his diaper is amusing, particularly if it is one of his first. A simple, natural process we adults take for granted becomes a vaudeville act for parents watching.

It is most entertaining when it emerges during play. The activity stops, and the smile or laughter freezes in mid air and then fades as though visited by some ghostly presence. There is a second for wondering what happened, why the activity stopped so suddenly. In the next second, facial muscles tense up and blood rushes to the face. The arms shoot out and stiffen; the hands clench and their little knuckles begin to redden. Suddenly, all witnesses realize that something major is about to burst. The breath is held for an alarming second and the entire head gets red, including the very tips of the nose and ears. The little body tenses and bears down, and there is an almost anticlimactic little explosion in the diaper.

The entire body relaxes as soon as breathing resumes. Blood drains from the face, and the familiar color returns to the cheeks, forehead and ears. As suddenly as it stopped, activity picks up with hands and feet pumping in all directions. What follows is a look of surprise on his little face, sometimes alarm, sometimes even fear. Sometimes the shock of it is too much to bear, and the crying begins. The look of surprise, that clueless look, is most amusing for those looking on at the spectacle. They know exactly what just happened. The only one in the dark is the little culprit himself. In sight and hearing of all around, some of whom he has just a passing acquaintance, he has done what is not done in polite company, and he makes no apology. Instead, he has a look upon his face as though he was quite innocent and had no idea where it all came from. The boldness of this display of absolute innocence is what is so memorably comedic.

An infant's crib becomes the entertainment center for the family. It is the first place a returning father rushes to, and it is the place that captures most of mother's attention, love and concern. It is the place where the day is opened with the bouncing of bed springs, squeals, delightful murmurings, the music of the mobile and silly sounds, and it is the place where the day is closed with warm nourishment, whispers of endearment, gentle caresses and tender kisses.

If you were a hapless guest, it is the place where you would be invited to stand overtly in admiration. It is where you would hear incessant conversation about nothing else but the baby. You would hear it whether you wanted to or not. At no time would much attention be paid to you or anything you may be saying not relevant to the baby. It is all about the baby. It is a place where many firsts occur, and the sounds, the images and the expressions that result have a firm grip on our funny bone and the strings of our hearts. There is no entertainment like it; at least, not in the perception of those in the loving circle that envelops the crib. Here, entertainment is free and plentiful, and all have front row seats.

There is wonderment in staring at a grinning infant in a crib, flailing at the empty air with all limbs pumping in opposition to each other, seemingly striking at the brave new world thrust before him. There is endless amusement in watching him discover his left arm, then his right, his nose and then his mouth and react as though the discovery would bring unremitting applause; to watch him move all his limbs about with ostensibly little control; to see the puzzlement in his face at all of it; to see his hand hit himself in the face and to see him recoil in genuine surprise as he ponders where the blow came from and seemingly braces for another.

When they discover their feet for the first time, it is inserted into the mouth. How they are able to get it in the mouth is amazing to all the watching adults whose bones have set and whose ligaments have hardened. They are like little toothless mimes in stinky diapers titillating the tenderest parts of us all.

And their faces, as they wake from a sound sleep, have all the curiosity of looking for the first time into the monitor of an old computer seconds after it's turned on: "checking memory," then "checking peripherals," then "checking modem." Not infrequently, their countenance freezes. There is a blank, blinking stare "C:/...." Despite all the key strokes and mouse movements, nothing happens. The life in their eyes begins to slip away moments after the first jostle. The visage begins to dim like the screen of a monitor thirsting for an input, but there are no screensavers. They need to be rebooted, sometimes by a gentle nudge, a voice, a kiss on the cheek, a less gentle nudge, a louder voice. If the rebooting is not well-done, the rest of the morning is met with sluggish performance, slow responses to commands and sometimes a total failure of all circuits.

There is a wondrous distraction when your own child, wearing nothing but his diaper, crawls on the floor finding adventure even in the fibers of the carpet, a place where most adults are not likely to find anything of interest. Unless one is gravely out of sorts, one would not sit for long minutes in a soiled diaper, and while drooling, take so much curiosity in the fibers of the living room carpet. Yet something of amazement seems to fix his attention for long minutes, and while you are wondering what could possibly be going through his mind, it happens before you can move a muscle. Whatever it was that seemed to have held his interest for so long goes into his mouth. Just as quickly, you are off from your relaxed, sedentary position. You frantically slosh through his toothless mouth to retrieve it, and to your relief it finally comes out in the drool. Sometimes the object of so much interest is never revealed. Despite the fright and the ordeal, he rewards you with a mischievous smile as though saying, "Well, you got that one, but just wait for the next one... and the next."

I dare anyone to conduct an adult conversation with the parent while such an event is unfolding. If you want verification of this, ask anyone who has visited parents of young children. Couples who were constant social companions at one time and who engaged in intelligent, free-flowing and witty conversation on all manner of issues, become distant from each other after one couple has a child. The minds of parents who have a child are distracted; their minds are always on their child. Their world has changed. Their interest now is not about themselves or weighty political or philosophical questions, but about the welfare of a little one who had exploded into their world. One minute they were a couple; the next minute they are a family. They have become members of a privileged, exclusive and esoteric club where all members are joined inextricably like a mat woven by love from the fibers of their lives.

Watching an infant explore his or her new world is like staring into the fireplace. We can stare endlessly into a fireplace, lost in our thoughts and forgetful of lingering worries. It is a soothing, relaxing distraction. In that same way, we can get lost in cherubic faces. What thoughts are dancing in their heads to cause that playful little smile that appears so unexpectedly and for no apparent reason?

What is behind Da Vinci's Mona Lisa smile has for decades filled otherwise empty time in art and social circles around the world, yet minute by minute and day by day, in the faces of infants and little children, there flash quizzical expressions that Mona Lisa would envy. Parents can debate endlessly about that smile and wonder about that grin. What is the meaning of that smile that disappears as suddenly as it appears? Where does it come from? What thoughts or dreams provoke it? Even in their sleep, in their cribs or beds, this show marches endlessly on. Smiles, grins and emotions pass over their sleeping faces at night, challenging us with wonderment. We do not just wonder about the expressions on little new faces; we wonder too about why we find so much enjoyment in wondering about them.

In an Infant's Face

What for, Mona Lisa, do you smile?
Paint on canvas is all,
Yet the world is enthralled,
And all are intrigued for awhile.

Guesses abound in tuxedos and gowns,
At parties and galleries,
With champagne, wine and canapés,
Not a wink, not a hint can be found.

In faces of infants, all sorts of expressions to
guess on
There are smiles and grimaces,
All manner of faces,
What for do you smile? What for did you grin and
frown?

Just now what for? Just then, why then did you
smile?
Neither canvas nor paint constrains,
The excitement or wonder contained
In the love of an infant's smile.

Everything this stranger does is an event, even if the events are worrisome, full of fear, full of anxiety. For included are moments of indescribable warmth, happiness and joy. Suddenly, life is eventful; life is full and purposeful. The world and all its seemingly insurmountable problems are reduced to a single crawling infant searching the carpet for novel sensations. The looks that play on their little faces at each new discovery send a thrilling reminder to us of the many things we have taken for granted, because we have allowed them to become commonplace. Their faces have become a mechanism for us of

---

rediscovery, an opportunity to reacquaint ourselves with the once familiar but forgotten.

Maybe, it is a reminder of when we were children and the whole world was fresh, new and exciting. A bath in a tub of warm water becomes an odyssey of sensations for us, vicariously through their expressions. First there is the suspense revealed by the initial rigidity of the body when she first touches the water; then there is the fear that seizes her face as she is gently lowered into the water. As the fear passes, a guarded smile appears in response to the enveloping warmth. Our eyes are fixed on her face at every stage as we hope to be thrilled with the next expression that visits it. As they become less intimidated by the splashing of water, more secure in our grasp and pleased at the water's warmth, activity picks up and the bathtub becomes a playground of novel experiences for both parent and child, soaking the floor, the counter, the mirror, the medicine cabinet and the amused parent.

If children were not so irresistible, we would certainly throw them out. That they are irresistible is Nature's way of assuring that the welcome mat for these strangers is always out.

For years, science has attempted to come up with an explanation of the "cuteness factor." In my mind, however, there is a price to be paid for everything; nothing is without cost. When we become too immersed in trying to understand something, we may lose the wonder and pleasure of it. To study why and how music inspires and moves us can detract from the enjoyment of the music. There is a difference between those who attempt to analyze art to understand it and those who simply enjoy and/or create art. Astonishment, surprise, suspense and mystery are all casualties when the method of the magician is revealed before the act. As it is sometimes said, "To understand it, is to lose the meaning."

How then did I treat you differently? There were many ways, some too subtle for even me to know. I sought out that femininity in many ways... I didn't have to do much for it. It came with no strings attached and no extra energy. It draped itself around me when I sat down to read the newspaper or to watch television. It jumped into my bed when I tried to close the day. In many ways, it seemed that it sought me out, and that was even more endearing. Because I enjoyed it, I tended to spend more time with you. At the end of a long day, I may have been less inclined to throw ball with your brother, but with you could just sit in my chair and you would be content just hanging onto my neck or listening to my heart beat... You just wanted a safe comfortable place to stay. Nothing was required of me. I am sure your brother sensed it and knew he could not do the same; he could not compete. I was conscious of this possibility and so I tried never to go without hugging and kissing him. Give one something he yearns for and he will be more generous, so I think you got more of my attention.

Perhaps, psychologists will come up with some scientifically satisfactory explanation why it is that it is so much more soothing and comfortable to watch a little girl prim herself before a mirror after taking a bubble bath than to watch a little boy splashing in a tub trying to sink an armada of toys. I'll leave it to them to tell us why to a father it is so much more hypnotic to watch little girls fuss with their clothes and their stuffed dolls than it is to watch a little boy wallow in a mud hole. Maybe, it is because boys need a respite from the games boys play. I for one think that to find the answer is to lose the meaning.

When I was a kid, I wondered how the food was processed after I ate it and even why it came out in such a disgusting form. I thought and thought about it. I came to imagine that there was a little person inside me that was eating this food and passing it through for me. There, I thought, that solves that problem. I felt good about that answer to the enigma. I was content. I was satisfied with the resolution of that puzzle until I grew a little older and it occurred to me to ask how the food was processed after the little person inside me ate it.

As I think back on it, I was very content and at peace with the first resolution of that problem. I was disturbed when I began to question it. Learning and growing up is inevitable, but there was a price to pay for growing up. Children tend to be more at home in a world that amazes though they cannot understand, and in that world, adults, who have forgotten their childhood, may feel unwelcome. But little strangers welcome their parents and make their parents' entry into their world possible. Through our children, we live again.

CHAPTER THREE

Squeaks, Big Eyes, Etc.

Heart bumps jogger, and "daddy made doo doo.".

Children do and say silly things. My little daughter, Kelly, handed her mother a brightly colored Band-Aid saying, "Mommy, hold this while I go outside and fall down." Band-Aids were intended for minor injuries. The companies that produced them put colorful designs on them to comfort a child and raise their spirits. Children, however, had other plans. Why wait for the injury? Skip that. It may never happen, and besides, there was pain associated with it. Children are smarter than that. Colorful Band-Aids are a badge of honor. They stick whether there is an injury or not. They stick whether there is pain or not. They stick in any case, at all times of the day and for any occasion. It is much easier to skip the undesirable preliminaries and go right to the honor.

I was at the gym to increase muscle mass and to maintain my already fabulous physique. I was doing some bench presses. The trainer came over and said, "Ahmmm. You know. You should increase the weights if you expect to get any benefit from that exercise." Taking my cue from the Band-Aid incident, I heard myself saying, "That would be foolish. If I increased the weights, it would be harder to push it off my chest." There is humor and joy in the reasoning of a child even when it intrudes into adult situations.

As my children were growing up, they saw that their father would often put on running shorts and shoes and jog through the neighborhood. This was not lost on little Kelly. It must be fun, she must have thought. She wanted to do it too. She wanted to do it with her dad. She must have thought it to be an adult thing, and she wanted to do what adults do. So one day when she noticed that I was preparing to go out again, she looked up at me and said, "Daddy, I want to go with you."

Her legs were too short to even keep up with me, and so I tried to discourage her at first. I needed to get some cardiovascular benefit by maintaining a fast pace, and I knew I was not going to get it if she accompanied me. Fortunately, I also thought to myself that this would be a good father-daughter opportunity, so I dropped my initial protest and asked her to get her socks and shoes. A lot of time and a lot of patience were expended to find the socks and then the shoes and then to put them on her little feet, but at last, we were ready.

I started to do some stretching exercises, and so did she. At least, she went through the motions not having any idea what the purpose was. She had seen me doing it many times in the past. Her father was doing it so she was going to do it. She watched me and then placed her outstretched arms with palms up against the building, feigning to stretch first her right and then her left leg. She was going through the motions imitating me, except her little legs were bent at the knee when they should have been stiffened. No amount of stretching was actually occurring. As she spread her feet far apart she kept faltering and losing her balance. It was a sight that only a father could treasure, a little daughter falling all over herself trying to imitate what her father was doing, but with no understanding of the purpose and certainly with no efficacy.

Kelly was pretty and devilishly cute from the moment of her birth, and the shock of black hair she was born with made her even cuter. To my dismay, she lost the black and now had a full head of dark brown hair cut just above her shoulders. Between her and Erin, she was the closest thing to being a daddy's girl. She was always happy to see me when I returned at the end of the day and she was always the one who sought me out and insisted on my hugs and kisses. I was totally enchanted. The effect of her charm on me was so complete that I often felt I was her emotional captive when she wrapped her arms around my neck. Her femininity brought home to me, like nothing else, the difference between a little boy and a little girl.

When Kelly was in college she asked me if I had ever treated her differently from her brother because she was a girl.

How did I treat you differently from your brother? That is hard to say. Did I treat you differently because you were a girl as opposed to a boy? That's difficult to know. I can definitively say, however, that I did treat you differently. Why I did so can only be known intuitively. You were so delicate, so small, so tiny and so fragile. You were so little that when I held you to my chest, I barely knew you were there. This may account for different treatment shortly after you were born. Remember that picture of you in a big pot on the stove? We handled you as though you were a delicate piece of glassware. Of course, too, you looked different from your brother and sister when they were infants. They looked more alike at that age. You had black hair that stood up on your little head and you had this expression as if to say you couldn't wait to get into things. It was a look of mischief and inquisitiveness that seemed to always linger on your visage. And when you smiled, it seemed to play over that look; it was like a knowing smile that sometimes turned into a cute grin that threatened to break your cheeks. And when you cried, your little body would shiver with the need for something to be done.... your whole face turned red and your whole body would tighten as though you were contracting all your muscles, as a body builder would to impress the judges. And then there would be this brief silence as though you were catching your breath and building up to another huge squeak....except for in the middle of the night, this was cute to behold. So your crying may have had the opposite effect....it did not always get the intended response from us. It is difficult to put aside all these cute and endearing traits in order to ascribe any difference in treatment solely to your gender. But....it cannot be denied that there is something in girls that garners special affection and tenderness from a dad, but I feel I must cite memories of you beyond the infant stage to supply the proof.

As a little girl you were charming and endearing, soft, delicate and warm; you were feminine. You were feminine in the way you tossed your hair to the side and combed it, in the way you nuzzled up to me on the bed, in the way you caressed your teddy bears and asked inane little questions. Femininity is probably the best word for it. It is intoxicating to men. It is, perhaps, a quality shunned today by more and more women, but it *was a quality that was naturally there from birth, and you had it in abundance. It is softness, tenderness, warmth, a quality of caring and of need for warmth returned, a gentleness of manner and spirit and of thought, a breezy movement, a tender assurance, a look of concern when hurt is felt, a pat on the back of the hand and an understanding shoulder. Femininity is an aphrodisiac not just to boys and men, but to hard-working fathers at the end of the day. It is something that your brother, thankfully, did not have. It is not seemly for men to have, but it is a quality that holds men captive and makes them slaves to a beauty that fades. It is a quality that men hunger for.... Maybe in the study of little girls and their fathers lies the answer to some of society's problems. Maybe, a little girl with shiny eyes, long flowing hair, unquestioned love and trust in her ways satisfies that hunger. For a dad, a little girl is a special gift."*

Soon I was ready to begin my jog. I asked little Kelly if she was ready.

"Yes, daddy." she said in her sweet, squeaky voice.

I trotted slowly down a slight slope to the nearest corner. To keep up, she had to sprint down alongside me. To my left and below my shoulder, her little head bobbed at my side. This was going to be so great, I thought.

When we reached the corner, certainly no more than 50 yards from where we started, she stopped suddenly and announced, "Daddy, stop. I don't want to go."

I was surprised; we had traveled such a short distance. After having gone through all the preliminaries, I had to ask, "Why?"

Looking up at me, wrinkling her nose and wiping her forehead with her forearm as though she had just jogged a mile, she replied, "Daddy, it is making my heart bump. I don't like my heart to bump."

After gathering myself together from a fit of laughter that brought tears to my eyes, I walked her back to the house. I resumed my jog through the neighborhood with the welcome weight of an unrelenting smile that intermittently broke into laughter and that laughter threatened to trip me up and break my stride.

Most of us tend to be goal-oriented. Enjoyment of our quests in life depends in part upon how we see that goal. A child's goal is often different from an adult's; how we see it colors our perspective. We can apply this instruction when taking a vacation. Adults fix their minds on getting to the destination; they confuse getting there with the real goal. The primary goal of a vacation is to have fun and relax, to spend quality time with each other. Children don't want to wait; they want to enjoy the trip. The primary goal is not the destination. Adults focus on the destination; children live for now. Children want to enjoy the trip as well. Focusing solely on their graduation from college can result in missing everything in between. Life can be a trip or it can be a destination. The trip may be longer than the stay at the destination. There is much to learn from that distinction. Children remind us that life should be both a trip and a destination. We learn about life from the unlikeliest places, even from children.

The years go by in a blink of an eye. In a blink of an eye my college life is over. In the blink of an eye my children have grown into young wonderful adults. In the blink of an eye I am watching them graduate. Soon, in a blink of an eye I will watch my children get married and in a blink of an eye I will be a senior citizen. After many blinks, I have learned and become wiser and want very much to impart that wisdom to my children. Enjoy the interlude between each blink. Savor it. Relish it. Remember to enjoy the trip to your objective and goals in life. The trips can last longer. The objectives and goals, once achieved, can last but a short time. It is a message that bears constant reminder.

I am glad that you love college. Sometimes, I guess, I need reminding. You seem to be so focused on the future. You seem so anxious to get there, so impatient with the present and so driven to get somewhere else. Your ambition seems to drive the present out. One day you will be visiting your college campus as an alumnus, and your college times will be but a dream, a longing and an aching. If you fill your moments with activities in preparation for the future, it is impossible to enjoy the moments you have. The moments you have now are yours and in your hand; moments in the future may never come. Moments now are real; you can count on them. Moments in the future can only be wished for.

Carol baked a delicious-looking cake. Not long after it was baked, little Erin had her eyes on it. She seemed almost able to taste the sweetness passing over her tongue on its way to her wanting, waiting tummy. She asked to get it into her mouth. Carol told Erin, "The cake is for later." That seemed to pacify her, but it seemed too easy. In response to Erin's persistent and many inquiries during the day, her mother repeated that the cake was for later. After awhile, my daughter asked, "Mom, who is Later, and why does he get everything?"

It is amusing to imagine how little Erin may have felt throughout the day. Who was this person that her mother just referred to? Was she really expecting Later to walk through the door? Was she looking out for him? Were her thoughts bothered through the afternoon why mother favored Later over her to eat the cake? Whoever Later was, since he got the cake, Erin would have benefited greatly from making Later her playmate. Enjoying the cake with a new friend would have been something to be looked forward to. All are humorous to think of. A trip through the mind of a child is a source of infinite amusement.

It is as much a challenge to explain the concept of time to any three- or four-year-old as it is to explain the concept of stranger to a little boy skipping in the neighborhood. Picking up the challenge and following through can become anything a parent chooses to make of it. It can become a wondrous and amusing trip through the fresh and untouched mind of a child. It is an opportunity parents can choose to take or not, but trips take time and too often we have so little of it. Someone who chooses to be a parent has such numerous opportunities light on their faces like warm raindrops.

My tenants terminated their lease and vacated their house. As is customary, they cleaned the house and removed everything they owned. Everything was removed from the refrigerator and it was thoroughly cleaned. I began to show the house to prospective tenants.

One day a young family of prospective tenants came by with their two little children in tow. The parents walked all over the vacant house while their children practiced to become Olympic gymnasts in the living room. While it is usually lost on most adults, these two had discovered a gymnasium in the now vacant living room. It was an opportunity to vent their excess energy. This empty space was an irresistible invitation for unsupervised play without the worry of parental intervention. It was a time for them to display the agility of youth. There were no pesky couches, chairs and tables that would obstruct acting out their fertile imaginations. There was nothing fragile to break. Twirls, somersaults, pirouettes and playful falling down, all accompanied by screams of glee, filled the living room.

Sometime after their parents had gone up to explore the second floor, the children realized their audience had gone and their remarkable athleticism was no longer being appreciated. There, of course, was no sense in knocking themselves out if there was no applause or appreciative eyes. Exhausted, they stopped their play. No longer preoccupied, they began to discern a grumbling in their stomachs. It was the unmistakable call that all children learned to respond to soon after the umbilical cord is severed. Except now, instead of responding to hunger by crying loudly and making a fuss, they had learned to make a polite request to any convenient adult. As it happens, I was convenient. Why not this gentleman? So they approached me; looked up at me and asked,

"Sir, we're hungry. Is there anything to eat?"

"No" I said in an apologetic voice. I was impressed by how polite they were.

"Mister, are you sure there is nothing to eat?" they asked again.

"Yes, I am sure." said I, now in a more sympathetic manner.

They remained silent for awhile looking at each other and then pleadingly at me. Then one of them said, "We are really hungry, Mister."

I said, "I'm sorry, but there is nothing to eat in the house. This house is vacant and for rent." They looked at each other and began to fidget uncomfortably. It became clear to me that those words, vacant and for rent, had absolutely no meaning to them.

They remained standing in front of me, fixed in place and fidgeting. They seemed not to believe me.

Then a thought occurred to me how I might dispel their seeming disbelief.

"Come" I said, and I took them to the kitchen and walked directly over to the refrigerator. I opened the refrigerator. As the door opened, the light went on and the cold air came rushing out. They peered into the empty refrigerator long enough for their young minds to realize that the refrigerator was totally empty -- no milk, no meats, no fruits, no vegetables, and no candy, nothing.

They looked at each other and fidgeted where they stood. As I puzzled over what may have been bothering them, they looked up at me. In a tone replete with sadness and pity, one of them asked, "Mister, are you poor?"

A neighborhood friend of Kevin's whom I had not seen for years, came over to our front door one day. When I saw him I said, "My, Alfred, you've grown a foot since I last saw you." Overhearing what I had said, Erin came running to the front door asking, "Where? Where? I want to see." She wanted to see the new foot that this boy had supposedly grown. In a flash, her little mind had conjured up the regeneration of a human limb, for in their minds all things are possible.

The minds of adults made rigid by life find it difficult to soar through the clouds and into limitless space like those of children, that is, until children give them the wings to do it. Perhaps, that is what dreams are about. When we sleep we dream of fantastic things, things that we would not dare think of when we are awake. I remember dreaming that my family came to see me at the airport and waved goodbye to me as I boarded the plane. When I arrived at my destination thousands of miles away, there they were to greet me as I disembarked. The rest of my dream was spent in frustration trying to figure out how they did it. Maybe it is that when our minds are free from the rigidity of thought imposed upon us by the realities of life, we become more relaxed, more rested. That may, indeed, be the ultimate purpose of dreams.

We would not have to put up with such silliness if they were not around, but then, just look what we'd lose. What happens when mothers and fathers cannot get lost in innocent eyes, laugh at genuinely quizzical looks that pop up in surprise on endearing little faces and feel the tug of unquestioning love and dependence?

When my son was just about three years old, a commotion occurred in his bedroom, and I rushed in wearing only my low-cut briefs. I appeared at the door just as Kevin was about to take flight into the next room. Outlined through the brief was that part of my anatomy that was, in part, to blame for the conception of my son. It was, of course, at Kevin's eye level as he was racing past me. He suddenly stopped in mid flight, like a road runner spying its prey. He fixed his eyes at the bulge for a second or two. I wondered why the motion in the room had suddenly stopped. As if to answer, he raised his arm and pointed at the bulge, and he shouted, "Mom, daddy made doo doo. Daddy made doo doo."

There is no price that can be paid for that moment, no amount of money; there is no comparable substitute. To laugh at something your own child says or does is like drinking hot soup with the laughter; it warms you from head to toe. Laughter too often is the medicine that we inadvertently find stored in a forgotten place in the back of the medicine cabinet. That moment seemed to touch me more deeply and tenderly because it issued from a three-foot-tall innocent child of my very own. It was my son expressing dismay that daddy's diaper had not been changed as his so often was since birth. Daddy needed mother's care. Registered in his little face was genuine concern for his father whom he saw as in distress. It had become an urgent matter to see to it that daddy would get relief.

I remember a time when I was in my office just days before a case was to go to trial. Much was hitting the fan all at once. I opened the telephone book to retrieve a number to make an urgent call. At that moment my paralegal came in and told me that certain case preparations were falling apart and needed my immediate attention. I stood up to follow him out of the office still carrying the phone book. At that very instant, my secretary came in and announced that a judge was on her phone demanding to talk to me. I reversed myself and started toward another phone, still holding the phone book which was still open to somewhere I had forgotten. Then the phone on my desk rang. I found myself taking a step toward yet another phone, then a step toward my secretary, and then toward my desk and then suddenly realizing that I still had the telephone book in my hands and had forgotten whose number I was searching for, I dropped the book and laughed hysterically. I was on the edge of the precipice and laughter pulled me back.

If you have ever gone to see a professional comedian perform, you will know that there are always some in the audience who do not catch on to a joke. In that second they may have missed an opportunity for laughter. Opportunities come and go in life. Sometimes we miss it and sometimes we don't. With children there are many such opportunities. We must be observant and on guard, not just for laughter, but for joy and tender moments. The loss of perspective is what distracts us and impedes our ability to remain on guard. The pull of the warmth and joy of the family circle is the anchor that helps us to resist the distractions. The very sad irony is that some of us resent that very pull.

We laugh and enjoy children because they evoke reminiscences of our own childhood and all of the fanciful thoughts that had amused us endlessly. I used to live in a very narrow lane, in a very small, single frame house. Behind that house was a trickling stream. A wooden bridge of heavy timber spanned the stream. As a child, I crawled and climbed all over and under that bridge, and in my mind must have blown it up a thousand times to halt the advance of the fearsome enemy. I saw many hostile soldiers and trucks, including tanks, plummet into the deep abyss of the canyon after the bridge creaked and groaned and finally gave under the weight. I had single-handedly saved my little neighborhood. I had done this many times. I was a hero many times over. I risked my own life over and over again. It was difficult and dangerous work that I gladly did to ward off the boredom of the long summer days.

When we laugh at our children, we laugh at ourselves. We see ourselves in our children, and we laugh. Memories of our own carefree days flood back into places in our brain we had forgotten. Children take the medicine out from the back of the medicine cabinet and give it a prominent position in our daily lives.

Disneyland was a place I always wanted to go to ever since I heard Walt Disney explain his dreams of building that "Happy Place" in Anaheim, California. I was not able to go until I was about 19 years old and in college, but when I did go, it was enjoyable. I am sure I would have enjoyed it even more if I had visited it when I was much younger. In a few short years, I was able to go to Disneyland several more times. Soon, the novelty disappeared and the magic in the Magic Kingdom was gone, and the rides seemed unexciting and boring.

When children came into my life, Disneyland was exciting again, but not through my adult eyes. As incredible as it may seem, I could see old things as new and exciting through my children's eyes. I had, it would seem, new eyes. What had grown stale and old was suddenly new, and Disneyland was definitely a place I had to return to. This time I would bring my children and I would bring my new eyes.

I now, however, had a job and a profession. Time became an expensive commodity. I sold my time to make a living, to provide for my family and to provide for our future. Time, however, was the same commodity that my children, my family required. Time, which once seemed so abundant when my imagination was blowing up bridges in my neighborhood, became scarce. What time I did not give to my profession or business had to be devoted to my family. So when I visited Disneyland, I needed to cram as many shows, activities and rides into the time allotted for my vacation as I possibly could.

My law office was on the twentieth floor of a very tall office building. It was immured by an external one-way glass wall extending from floor to ceiling. I had a large wooden desk at which I spent most of my time. I needed it to be large to lay out the many legal authorities, books and documents I usually used as source material when preparing legal briefs or memoranda. One day I noticed that the desk came very high up to my chest. This made it difficult for me to read the books comfortably. I thought to myself that I really needed to get a new chair, but I was too busy and my mind was too occupied to find the time to go out and buy another chair. Many times, off and on through the years, the thought of getting a new chair would plague my mind. I was just too busy to get it done. This went on for five years. I did not feel comfortable at my desk because the chair needed to be replaced. Then suddenly, after those many years, in a rare moment when I was sitting at my desk with nothing to do, another thought entered my head. It was a eureka moment. It was an uncommon voice in my head. It said, "Adjust the chair." My profession and business had been so frenetic and stressful for so long that that very simple solution never occurred to me until I was enjoying a moment of respite from the insanity of my law practice.

Most parents who have gone through the Disneyland experience with their children in tow will tell you that at that stage of their lives the park grounds stretched larger and longer as the hours of each day unfolded. There never was enough time; the lines were longer, the heat unbearable, the crowds more pressing, and the standing, waiting, pushing and rushing were more exhausting. We would spend more than nine hours a day in the park, on our feet and in long lines, rushing here and there and scurrying from one line to another. Why then did we do this? We did it because we were having fun. The rides and attractions that had become stale to me seemed newer, fresher and more enjoyable with my children. Instead of the first-hand thrill of the ride or attraction, it was their look of surprise, their squeals of delight and the happiness that those rides brought to their faces that made all worth it. Every expression of glee on their little faces was a personal high, every smile a boost of pure joy, and every first discovery a renewed discovery for us seasoned visitors. Now when Chip n' Dale made an appearance, the wonder and excitement in my children's eyes were mine, and we fought for every chance to make those smiles and chuckles reappear, just as we did when we tickled them in their cribs. Every time they did reappear became a camera-snapping opportunity. Watching my children's first experiences became my favorite pastime. Life was no longer just about us, it was about them, not just for them, but for us.

Five-year-old Kelly surprised me at the end of one exhausting day of long lines, feeding their hunger and visiting restrooms between shows and rides. With her little hand in mine as we stood outside of the park waiting for our ride back to our motel, Kelly, while barely propped up on her little legs, looked up at me with her weary eyes fixed on mine and observed: "Daddy, I can't believe what you are doing for us. Thank you." That such a little person could so appreciate the events of that day was confirmation to me that all was worth it. The pride of that moment was purchased by the exhaustion and chaos of that day. As a father whose mind was too often preoccupied with time, I had tried to hurry everything up so that my children would not miss a single minute of fun. The significance of all of our efforts was forgotten by me but not lost on my precocious five-year-old. That moment was the prize to carry with me for the rest of my days.

So what is it then that makes us love these little wrinkled strangers? I am not talking about puppy love; I am talking about real, genuine love, the kind of love that will cause us to lay down everything we own and possess, and our very lives for; the kind of love that makes our hearts soar when we perceive just the hint of a smile; the kind of love for which we are willing to stay up nights even though we are totally exhausted; the kind of love that draws a smile from us when we just hear a squeal; the love that makes us put up with dirty diapers, sleep-depriving screams, tossed food, copious drooling, incomprehensible gibberish; the kind that makes us bring them into our homes; provide them warm beds, and spend hard-earned money for clothes and food. What makes it so satisfying to see these little strangers fill their bellies and fall asleep in their mother's arms? With our troubles we purchase all those many moments when we must fight back tears of joy, tears that wash away the difficulties of raising them.

What is it about infants and little children that make us act like, well, little children? Before we know it, we start babbling like little children ourselves. We speak in very simple sentence fragments that would bring a blush to an English teacher's face. Childless couples, with whom we once spent so much time, suddenly feel lost in the obvious change in their friends. Married couples who once called each other such endearing names as "honey", "sweetheart" and "baby" discover one day that they are calling each other "mom" and "dad". We had lost our proper names. We make outlandish noises to get their attention, "goo goo", "gah gah" and other meaningless and ridiculous sounds. We mimic the mime in their crib, and in some cases we carry on this absurd behavior even after they are long grown and out of the house.

Maybe, it is because they are still our children, and we are still their parents. Our thoughts were always about them whether we were with or without them. Everything that was important about us was them. Nothing more consumed our minds and hearts than they. They had become us, and it was impossible to separate us from them. Their departure comes at a time when we are older and less capable of coping with the change. Maybe that is the reason we still hang on to the belief that they are still with us and that things have not changed; it is a way of softening the blow of their absence.

It could also be because they won't let us change. In a conversation with our then-adult daughter Erin, my wife referred to me by my proper name. Pausing briefly and seeming a little confused, Erin asked, "Who?....oh, you mean dad." So Carol went back to calling me dad.

Shakespeare asked what is in a name. After having raised children, I have concluded that there is a lot in a name. Poopsie, popskipoops, popskipoopsaroni, dad, daddy, father and parental figure are just some of the appellations I am now called by my children. Ma, momsie, mom-head, mommie, and mom are some of the salutations extended to their mother. Physicians are called doctors, so are Ph.Ds. In England, special titles are given to people whose extraordinary service is recognized by the Queen. Such titles are highly valued. In my mind, there is more value and meaning to the title of father and mother and all names given us by our children. I wear them with honor and with pride and would not exchange them for all the titles that Her Majesty could bestow on me.

When I'm in a crowd, at a mall, on the street or at a playground, I will sometimes hear a child's voice cry out "Dad." For a second I stop, then resist the urge to turn and respond, and then I wish that the call really was for me. As the years go by, that urge has diminished, but I still derive pleasure whenever I hear the voices of children calling out "Dad" or "Mom". Maybe, it is because it reminds me of happy days, or maybe, it is because I momentarily feel happy for that mom or dad.

They force such a smile on our faces that we are amazed at it. The lines of age are absent from their smooth, clear skin. The whites of their eyes are like new fallen snow; their corneas are clear, dark and unclouded. They are new. Their images so overtake us that our minds are bothered in the search for the source of such wonderment in all children. It is the reward offered parents for bringing children into the world. When we become parents we shift the center of the universe from ourselves to our children, and all those petty worries that were so important to us before, suddenly become irrelevant. We put all of our dreams into these little bundles. They allow us to live again, a second life so to speak, where we can now relive the joy of Christmas, Easter, high school, college life and so many other things that had been forgotten in our struggles to find our place in the world. We become concerned not about ourselves but about another. Children give us a focus, and this focus perspective, and all that we searched for when we were in our teens and twenties suddenly is found. That is the wisdom that living through the natural stations of life brings: Children give us an excuse to be children again.

There is no one answer to the question of why we love little strangers. There are many answers, one being that they are not and never have been strangers. My wife and I met them in our courtship. We met them when we met each other. We got to know them when we got to know each other. We saw them in each other's eyes. During all of that time they were in design, and so when they finally came, we met ourselves in them. That, I surmise, is the reason why a man and woman take so long and put so much effort into finding a mate. All the materials and all the ingredients are there for the mixing long before the stranger is born.

There is magic in children. I have made an awkward attempt to describe that magic. One day in 2007 a little girl named Connie Talbot appeared on a TV show called "Britain's Got Talent." Several clips of her singing were posted on the Internet. There on YouTube was the evidence of the magic of children that I have struggled so hard to describe in words. Although the how and why of it is difficult to explain, the existence of that magic was evident in the effect of it, and that effect had been captured and memorialized on the Internet, websites, hard disks and DVDs.

The moment this precocious little figure of a child was carried on the stage by her little legs she enchanted everyone in the audience. The effect was palpable. Huge smiles were on the faces of everyone in the audience, and a murmur rippled through the theater followed by a hush as everyone strained to hear this little apparition speak. When she spoke in her little voice, so boldly and with the innocence of her childhood, an audible gasp rippled through the audience and smiles widened. Notwithstanding that the venue was a serious contest of talents being broadcast nationally and much was at stake for the contestants, a child melted the hearts of even the judges. A child had woven her magic. They were under her spell. The effects of her magic were clear for all to see. It was undeniably written in the faces of the audience and judges. It was written in the unison of smiles and in the hush and delighted gasps of hundreds of adults watching her performance.

Its effects were not limited to the immediate audience. Her magic spilled over to a nation and a global audience of those who watched on television and on the Internet. To google Connie Talbot would result in hundreds of hits all over the world, perhaps the best indicator of how widespread was her magic.

I was not spared the spell of her charm. I was so moved I wrote the following letter to the editor of our local newspaper.

Performance of Connie Talbot, a Child

A precocious and very talented six-year-old girl, whose permanent teeth had not yet set in, took the stage of a popular television program called Britain's Got Talent and blew away the competition. Connie Talbot was only a little less than three feet tall with long straight hair and a winning smile that could melt a glacier. All of the less than three feet of her bounced onto the stage before the delighted eyes of hundreds of people. Before she even sang a note, the sight of her standing alone so boldly before a panel of adult judges and holding a microphone that seemed so outsized in her little hands, caused an unmistakable murmur of surprise and rapture. Smiles were everywhere, the kind of tenacious smiles that seem to strain all the little muscles in your face. The audience was charmed by her innocent responses to some of the questions put to her by the panel of judges. When she began to sing, everyone held their collective breaths, and as each note rang in almost perfect pitch, one after the other, the tension soared for fear that she might falter, and it finally burst out into a relief of wild enthusiasm, tears and applause when the last note was sung as sweetly as the first.

What happened? What was so remarkable about her performance? Sure, she was talented, and she could sing on tune and she could sing well indeed, but her voice was naturally sweetened by the lilt of her childhood. She was adorable and lovable, huggable and kissable.

She was everyone's child. She had won before she had even begun to sing; for her voice did not and could not have had the finesse, the maturity, the polish and skill of a seasoned singer. She won by winning the hearts of her audiences, not as much by her talent as by her childhood.

Thank you, Connie, for reminding us of the blessing of having children. Your parents' pride and tears of joy requite the so-called difficulties of parenthood. Somehow we had forgotten that the joy of children is its own reward and that that reward is beyond compare.

Connie's performance, and more importantly, that of her adult viewers, can be seen on YouTube. You can also google Connie Talbot. Go there if you dare to endure tears of joy.

The real significance of Connie's performance was not just that she provided proof of the magic of children. The global reach of her magic was inarguably evidence that no matter what our disagreements and our nationality, all people of this planet were joined together in a brotherhood of human beings. Despite our differences, we are all affected alike by the faces of cherubs. It all became evident through the magic of a child that was televised around the world.

Carol and I had saved and managed our money and planned for the day our children would go to college. So when the day finally came, like so many other families, we would participate in the excitement of it by accompanying them to campus on the first days before school opened. We helped them check in and settle into their dormitory rooms, made sure that they had sufficient clothing and spending money, assured ourselves that they were safe, secure and comfortable, visited the buildings and grounds of their new campus and met some of their new friends and companions. Then we departed, leaving them behind for the very first time in their lives, but even more significantly, for the very first time in our lives.

Leaving them behind was difficult. It was the first time that they would be away from us for months at a time since they were born. We were anxious. Thoughts of their safety in their new environment, anxiety and sadness took hold of me. I had been planning this day since their birth, yet I felt incomplete. It was like planning a party, making the arrangements, preparing the food and drinks, putting up the decorations and then leaving without attending and enjoying the party. I became determined to be more of a participant, but not an intrusive one.

At a later time, I stayed with Kevin in his dorm room for a few days. I followed him to his classes, audited lectures, talked briefly with his professors, met and socialized with his friends, watched him study, shadowed him around campus, witnessed the new academic and social life he was living in and got out of his hair when he needed his own time. It was a marvelous experience, for in that time I was able to pretend that I was a student again and revisited the experiences and old haunts of my college life including the place where I had proposed marriage to his mother. It was exciting. In that brief window of time I was able to enjoy the party.

While he lived away from us in college I could now envision what he was doing, the friends he was spending time with and the environment he was in. When we spoke or wrote to each other, I was able to put his communications in context.

I wanted to tell you how happy I was to see you so artfully playing the ukulele and singing your heart out. I was delighted to see how gently and lovingly you held your friends and how gladly they returned your affection. I was pleased to see you before a group holding up so confidently and with so much humor. If there were any fears I harbored that you will not be happy, they were dispelled this summer. Your shyness has gone, and in its place is confidence and humility, and from that is charisma and leadership. People respect those who possess maturity and wisdom and sensitivity and philosophy above their own. You have all these qualities and more. They shine through you more so now that your shyness no longer disguises them. I am truly proud of you.

I did the same with Kelly and Erin, staying a few nights in their dormitory rooms or apartment. I got to know their friends, the walks they took most mornings from class to class, the cafeterias they ate in, the libraries, the classrooms and the places they sometimes visited. I became acquainted with their friends, their busy schedules, and the churches, organizations and Christian groups to which they belonged. I was able to allay any fears I may have had about their security and the quality of their environment and education. I was able to pretend I was a college student again. Now, when they talked about their friends, their professors and the places they visited I could see all of it in my mind's eye.

Now, at least, I could come to terms with their becoming young adults, their growing up, and their independence from their mom and dad. It was the beginning of my coming to terms with the pain of their long absence from home and my own insecurities.

I yearn for those times when I rocked in an overstuffed chair with the naked infant on my bare chest, so close that she could hear my heart beat. There is something overpowering about that moment as we felt and shared the warmth of each other's body and our hearts seemed to beat in unison. Eventually, I could not hear two, but only one heart beat. We floated together as in warm water, in and out of sleep, no longer feeling our separateness. I do not know what it was, but there was music made then, but I think, it was only heard by the two of us. No one outside of our warm private circle could hear our conversation or share the warmth and tenderness of that intimacy. It was transforming. It was immensely satisfying to have the little heart of my child communing with mine. Although she did not speak, I would have sworn she did; I did not hear it, but I felt every word just as one feels music though the lyrics are unintelligible.

My children now are grown. I miss those years when they were younger, smaller, when they were infants and toddlers. I wish I had not been so preoccupied with business. My profession demanded so much of my time and of my thoughts. Even when I was with them, my mind was always partially on my clients' matters, and it was not uncommon that issues about my cases would intrude to rob me of my time with them. It was the worst kind of theft, one that made me absent although I was seemingly present with them. My profession was an ever nagging mistress, demanding continual proficiency and precision when the law was anything but precise. It called upon me to keep current on the ever changing laws, to identify significant issues and to remember important facts. My wife would envy me at times because I worked in an adult world, and at the end of the day she yearned for adult conversation. My business required a lot of traveling and she saw it as exciting. On the other hand, I had grown tired of living out of suitcases and strange hotel rooms and continually bickering with opposing parties. I was jealous of her because she could spend more time with the children. I missed seeing them during and at the end of my work day, and I sometimes missed putting them to bed.

I tried desperately to spend more time at home particularly by getting home in time to put the kids to bed. Yet, to this day, I am not satisfied that it was enough time. I did not rush home at the end of the day for the children as much as I did for myself. I needed to spend time with them. I needed and hungered for the joy of their beguiling chatter, their inane questions, the warmth of their hugs and their kisses. They loved me despite all my flaws. They saw me as a tower of strength despite all of my weaknesses and perfect despite my imperfections. There were no preconditions for their love. The love and friendship of others may come from selfish motives and may be less than pure, but with your children there is no question that their love is real and pure. The end of my workday was the one opportunity every day for me to talk and play with them. They were the perfect medicine at the end of a trouble-filled day at the office.

There were times when I was late and they had already been put to bed. Feeling disappointed and unfulfilled, I would go up to their rooms and wake them up to get my dose of them. I knew it was selfish, but I could not help myself. Trying to wake up children at that hour of the night must be just like trying to roust hibernating bear cubs in the sanctuary of their cave. When I would do this they were so full of sleep that I am not sure they even remember much of what we said or did. Although this selfish act was frowned upon, I felt better after doing it. I thought that I had worked very hard to support them and the least they could do is put up with an occasional bedroom rousting.

There is something very special about hugging and kissing a sleepy-eyed child, just warmed all over from the covers, who is barely awake, feebly pushing away and trying desperately to return to his dreams, murmuring helpless protestations, and fighting to put off a father's kisses. It was a time when I could hold their warm bodies next to mine and while putting off their pleas to be left alone, make promises and confide in them problems at the office that they would not understand nor remember the next morning. Waking them up in such a fashion was unforgivable, of course. I will not lie. I did enjoy those episodes. I am glad I did it. I treasure the memories of those night-time bouts with them. I was the victor, of course, for I took advantage of them when they were most vulnerable. It was also a time when they were most cuddlesome. I have never felt guilt for those transgressions; I'd do it again.

When they were in college, I took many opportunities to write to them, especially with the advent of the Internet. Emailing was my way of giving them advice without seeming pushy or intrusive. Since I was not there, they could not see my demeanor; since they were not here, I could not see theirs. Somehow, the personal became less personally confrontational. If I gave advice, they did not have to pretend to hear it, consider it or accept or reject it. They could receive it without having to signal understanding or even agreement. Although I did not know whether they received it or understood it or benefited from it, I felt better about having written it and having sent it. Clicking that mouse was therapeutic. It made it easier for me to give them advice and make comments about their lives without the consequences. When I felt a need to give advice, I did, and when I clicked it away it disappeared into cyberspace presumably wending its way to their computers. I had performed my responsibility as a father; I had scratched that incessant, busybody itch that all fathers are prone to suffer to their very last day. This writing is sprinkled with quotes from some of those emails and letters that I sent to my wife and children.

CHAPTER FOUR

Dough Boy, Fears, Tears

Laughter, joy, fears and tears bring forth a father.

The best gift you can give us in the remainder of our lives is to first be healthy, now and in the future. Secondly, be happy. Thirdly, be prosperous and successful in life.

Usually, this means being financially self-supportive and independent; it means building your own emotional support, family, to weather the inevitable storms of life; it means not ever taking your health for granted; it means always remembering that those you love and who love you are your most important assets; it means never mistaking praise and adulation and riches for the unconditional love of family. These things come only with perseverance and hard work.

Kevin was shy when he was growing up. When he was an undergraduate he would go to the computer lab and write emails to others whose identities he may not have known. Everyone, of course, had their own handle, or as it is called, email address, and their true identities were not always known. As Kevin told it, he would write to someone called "Tiger Lilly." He had never met her and had no idea who she really was. Apparently, this exchange of emails went on for quite a while. One day, somehow they both came to notice that the person to whom they had been writing was sitting right next to him or her in the computer lab. Without exchanging a word, their first response was to sit back down at their respective computers and resume pounding at the keys to communicate with each other via email. Kevin would carry this shyness into his adulthood, but time, maturity and experience have noticeably chipped away at his shyness, but to a father impatient for his son's success, the erosion of that shyness seemed painfully slow.

There was one physical aspect of Erin that so charmed me; it was her big eyes. Those eyes seemed to hover like two moons over chubby cheeks. When she was older, I wrote to Erin alluding to her big eyes.

It is not possible anymore for me to hold your eyes with my gaze. Those big eyes now wander. They are restless and on the go; there is not time for letting a father stare too long into them. There are things to see with those eyes. There are places to take those eyes. There are many joys, sorrows, happiness and disappointments for those eyes to behold. There is your life to live and not much time to let a father's longing lips linger anymore on soft dimpled cheeks. It is a change that saddens me, for now as I move into the shadows you must step forward into the lights of the stage. My time for the big play has faded. Your time to shine is here.

Let the sadness of your father be your instruction. As we support you and applaud with pride as the curtains are raised and lowered on each performance, remember those in the shadows. Remember that at some time all of us must move off the stage. Remember this so that each moment the curtains go up you will savor your time. Remember to kiss the soft dimpled cheeks of your children. Remember to always gaze into their eyes and tell them "I love you." Do it as often as you can for too soon you will move into the shadows and they into the light.

Everyone speaks with praise and awe about maternal instincts when mothers become mothers, but little is said about the instincts of fathers when they become fathers.

Kevin was the first to be born. He made his appearance in the maternity ward of Kaiser Hospital where now stands the Hawaii Prince Hotel. He announced his approach in the early evening, but his arrival was delayed until the morning of the next day. The first time I saw him was when, with umbilical cord still attached, with a sudden sweep of the doctor's arms, my newborn son was laid on his mother's stomach before my amazed eyes in the delivery room. Almost as suddenly as he arrived, despite my protests, he disappeared into the arms of some of the attending nurses and the pediatrician.

Soon after the birth, they began quickly to attend to the mother and I was taken to wait for my son in another room. I was ushered into a large, very cold, air conditioned room, and they promised that they would bring him in. No one else was in the room. The room was quiet save for the loud whisper of the air conditioner. I could almost hear my breathing and my heart racing above the rush of air from the vents in the ceiling. About 20 minutes later a nurse appeared through the door wheeling in a stainless steel incubator with glass walls. As quietly as she came in and without even a word, she left the room. I thought her action was rude given that this occasion called for some a celebration or at least an acknowledgement, a hand shake or even just a smile of congratulations.

There seemed to be no world, no reality outside of that room. My whole world was in that room. It was as though that nurse left a time warp behind her as she closed the door and I was left alone with him. It was just me and this little stranger in the solitude and coldness of the room. A chill and excitement went through me. He was so tightly wrapped in a blue blanket that it would have been impossible for him to move his arms and legs. Only his head could be seen. He occasionally pursed his lips or wrinkled his brow. Sometimes I perceived a faint, fleeting smile as though something humorous had occurred to him in his dreams. He had been cleaned up and he was pink all over his face and head. The blue I saw in his face when we first met in the delivery room was nowhere to be found. His eyes were mere slits and barely opened and he did not seem to see me. He was perfect!

It had been in the delivery room when the doctor had placed him on his mother's stomach still blue all over that I had been taken by an intense emotion. The excitement and expectation had been building and the pace of the pushing and heavy breathing picked up with the gentle but firm entreaties of the doctor and nurses. The doctor, exclaimed, "There's the head." And then, "It's a boy." There was an exhalation of relief from the mother followed by a release of tension in the room. With a quick sweeping motion that seemed a blur, there he was on Carol's stomach. It was an almost unbearable crescendo of emotions. Tears welled up, strained against any resistance and then burst forth from me. They were tears that seemed to wash away whoever I was before; they were tears that brought in a bright new life. Carol and I looked at him and at each other through our tears. It was like looking through a window pane as rain drops ran down the outside of it. My wife had given me a son. Carol was exhausted and spent. I was so grateful for all she went through to bring this baby into our hands. I was so proud of her. I was so proud of him. I was still in that state then when I moved into that cold room. I remained in that room in that state all alone, waiting, until the door opened.

It seemed to me that he appeared in that room with stealth for I heard nothing, not even the opening of the door, the squeaking of wheels or the footsteps of the nurse that pushed him in. It seemed to me as though time had stopped. I heard nothing except my thoughts, my heart beat and my shallow breathing. I took each breath as though I feared the next one would dissolve everything that had just transpired. I was all alone with this little stranger. It was my time. It was our time. For long minutes, I stared silently at him through the glass window. Struggling alone with the wonder of it, I searched for the first words I would speak to this very little guy who an hour ago did not exist and whom I met just half an hour ago, and whom, as suddenly as he came, I loved.

I said, "Hello, little boy. I am your father. Welcome to the world." I know. Not very original or creative, but it was all that my brain could muster. There was no response, just slight movement of his head. I spoke in a whisper. I don't know why I did for there was no one else around, no one else to hear a word I said. It just seemed the right thing to do for this was our first conversation. I wanted to speak gently to him for my words were probably the first he would hear. The words were not for anyone else but him. The words and the promises I would make were for his ears alone. It was a special moment, a time of joy and a once in a life time conversation. Somehow, it seemed to me, the moment would be shattered if others could hear what I spoke. I continued to speak in a whisper which could hardly be heard above the humming of the air conditioner, except perhaps, by the little infant on the other side of the glass.

My face was less than a foot away from his. If he had the sight to see me, I think my face would have been very threatening to him. I revealed his name to him. No acknowledgement. He moved his head slightly and his tongue darted in and out. He seemed to taste the air with his tongue. I tapped on the glass to get his attention. No reaction. I continued by telling him that I would protect him and keep him safe. There was no response. I told him about all the experiences in store for him and the plans we had for him. Again, no response. I promised that I would take care of him and that he would get an education and go to college and make a difference in the world. Again, there was no response. There was not even a whimper or sound from him, and though he gave every indication of not having heard a single word I said, I held out the hope that he had heard me and understood what I said. But even if he did not, it made no difference to me. It was more important to me that I said those words to him than it was important that he heard them. No disruption, no distraction could have turned me away from that one-way conversation. It was just me and my son in that chilly room. I was having my very first conversation with my son, and I did not care about the problems of the office and of the world. It was our moment.

Of course, Kevin does not remember that one-way conversation, but it is one that thrilled me throughout and does to this day when I think about it. I felt connected to that room. I did not want to leave the room. I did not until someone came in and moved him out the door and the absurdity of my sitting in that room all by myself became too much to bear. It seemed to have taken a long while before I could recover from the disbelief that I had just had a meeting with my new-born son. When I left I was not the same person that had waited for his arrival; I had changed. I was more resolved and determined. My life seemed to be more purposeful. I was inspired.

So it was with the birth of both of my daughters. Prior to their birth, as with the birth of Kevin, we went to Lamaze classes to prepare Carol for the trials and challenges of childbirth. She did exercises to strengthen her abdominal and back muscles, and we were given instructions on how to help relieve her discomfort during labor. We received information on what the indicators for the baby's arrival were before coming in for admission to the hospital. Carol was always faithful to her exercises and diet. She took vitamins, calcium and fluoride to assure that the babies would be healthy, and she avoided second-hand smoke and other things that could endanger the baby. The maternal instinct was very powerful within her during her entire pregnancy, and it was evident by the glow that surrounded her.

While I slept through the night, Carol would bounce out of bed to attend to the baby as though knowing its needs before even the baby did. Sometimes I was conscious that she had just arisen. Although I felt guilty about not getting up with her, I persuaded myself that there was nothing I could do, really, to sate the roaring appetite of our baby. I did not have the equipment for it. I always needed seven to eight hours of sleep. It was difficult for me to be disturbed from my sleep. Nothing short of a firecracker exploding a foot from my ear could wake me.

There was a night when for no apparent reason I awoke from a sound sleep to find that Carol was not in bed with me. This was not unusual ever since the baby arrived. My getting up in the middle of the night was. When I awoke, it felt like I was slowly crawling out of a deep, deep dark well trying to reach for the light in the distance. I was still in my middle-of-night stupor, and I walked cautiously as in a dream. The room was dark. It felt as though I was walking in a dark tunnel, but there was a light streaming through the door, and my feet took me in that direction. I do not know why I awoke and I do not know why I walked toward the light. I seemed to walk with no purpose. I walked across the top landing of the stairway into the next room where I saw Carol with her long brown hair flowing down and across her shoulders. She was beautiful. She was sitting and very gently rocking in an orange rocking chair. She was wearing her blue night dress. Cradled in her arms and suckling on her breast was my infant son. In one hand she held an open book. As she rocked slowly back and forth, she was quietly humming a sweet tune, but over her humming I could hear my child contentedly sucking and drinking his mother's milk. Both were bathed by a soft light that seemed other worldly. I felt as though I was still dreaming and I had inadvertently broken into a beatific vision reserved only for the very blessed among us. It was a loving, private moment reserved mostly for a mother and a child, but often shared with a husband and father. It was an unforgettable and immensely satisfying sight.

About a year after Kevin's birth, I wrote this undelivered letter to my son. It tells how he had changed me, better, perhaps, than I can paraphrase it here.

Dear Son,

When you were just a little more than a year old, Mom and I went for a trek around the neighborhood. I slung over my back a blue canvas carrier with aluminum reinforcement. In there you were gently placed so that you could accompany us. You were so round then; your little dough boy body would not tolerate a single corner or angle. Your elbows and knees were so padded that it was difficult to imagine that they could bend.

The sun was shining that day. It was a glorious day. The smell of grass and dirt was in the air. The forest was lush and green, and the birds in the canopy of trees above our heads appeared to be celebrating the beauty of the day and singing to us on our walk. I had your pretty mother with me and my new son. I was so proud. Your fuzzy, oversized head bobbed up and down as I walked over the rough terrain on the path which had just recently been bulldozed behind our house. You seemed to enjoy the walk for I could hear you gurgle and make noises of perfect contentment as you looked all about you at the trees and blue skies while playing with a pacifier that we had given you. Occasionally, I would feel a gentle tug on my hair as though you were reminding me that you were there. You made that now familiar incoherent baby talk and incomprehensible mutterings as though you were having an intelligent conversation with yourself, and sometimes, it seemed as though you expected someone to answer you. Hearing you behind me filled me with satisfaction.

Then we came to a low lying area. It was a meadow covered by high grass. While walking through the grass, I stepped into a hole and lurched forward, but as I went forward I caught myself and stopped my forward progress. You lurched forward too, but your forward progress was stopped when your nose crashed against the back of my head. As I felt the collision, I froze for what seemed like long anxious minutes; I held my breath as it seemed the world and time had stopped. Suddenly, you cried out. Your pain and your cries pierced my heart. It seemed as though I felt your pain more than you did, and that moment, I knew that your birth had changed me forever. As I held back my tears and tried to assuage your hurt with soft words of comfort, I felt the pleasure of caring and of loving you.

The sun shone on all of us as we finished the hike, and I knew that the weight that I carried would, happily, be there long after I removed you from my back.

One day I heard Kelly screaming in pain. It sent a chill through me. I rushed into her bedroom to see her lying on her back on the bed while grasping her foot with both hands. Sticking in that little foot was a needle. About a third of it was embedded in her foot. She was screaming and rocking back and forth on her back. Tears were pouring from her eyes. I knew precisely what to do, but there was this inexplicable emotion that overcame me. I was terrified and angry at that needle. I felt as though that needle was sticking through my foot. How dare that needle assault my daughter? I was furious. I was murderous. Yet one must wonder about the sanity of any man who would direct such hostility at an inanimate object. It is not, after all, as though that needle could have formed a malicious thought to harm my daughter. Yet I felt as though that needle was an ungrateful guest in my home and that it had lain in hiding waiting for the opportunity to assault my daughter. To see such a rage in me, one would have easily been convinced that it was so, and that the needle was an intentional malfeasant. If that needle had taken on human form before me, it would have lived only a second after it took its first breath. I would have killed that needle. My murderous mood continued long after the crisis ended.

At a small neighborhood shopping mall, we were talking to a friend. My children were playing a few feet from us, jumping from place to place. Suddenly, I heard a noise that seemed to stop my heart in mid beat. I looked over. My little daughter, Kelly, had fallen head first onto the concrete walkway. I was relieved when she got up and seemed all right although a little dazed. As it happens our friend was a nurse. She warned us that we should keep an eye on her and if she should vomit we should take her immediately to the doctor for that could be a sign of a serious brain insult. Observing that she was all right I paid little attention to this admonition. When we returned home put Kelly back in her crib for her afternoon nap. She seemed so tired. When I later checked on her she lay sleeping in bed and to the side of her face was a large pool of vomit. Recalling my friend's admonition, I was suddenly seized with stark terror. This terror seemed to seize every part of my body. I woke her up and shouted to my wife that I needed to take her to the emergency room. The long trip to the emergency room, the x-rays and scans and medical procedures was a time of utter helplessness and fear. I was gripped by the horror of losing her of living the rest of my life without her. While she lay on the cold table being x-rayed, I stood by her side, with a lead apron draped over me, holding her hand.

Seconds before she had been born in the operating room, the doctor cried out that he could see her black hair. When she finally emerged into the bright lights, the nurses attending gasped and declared that she was the prettiest baby they had ever laid eyes on. Unlike Kevin and Erin who had a light fuzz of brown hair and who looked alike, she had a shock of black hair that stood out from her head. I had hoped that I would have at least one child who would have my black hair. She was small, very petite, fragile and cute, weighing less than 6 pounds. She was so slight, so tiny, so light, that her mother was able to put her into a stew pot. When she was on my chest I had to remind myself that she was there. She had this impish look of mischief on her little face as though she just could not wait to get into everything. On occasion she would seem to hold her breath as though to build up the necessary strength in her lungs to let out a cry, but it often fell short, and there would be a squeak instead. It was endearing to behold, fun to watch. She was very special and a precious little package of joy. I cherished the moments of holding her little body against mine. As the years passed, she continued to cling to me. She seemed to adore me and always sought my hugs and kisses before she went to bed, when I came through the door, for any reason, and at all times of the day. She was always working her feminine charms on her father, and I willingly gave in to them.

Not understanding all the commotion around her in the hospital, she looked up at me from where she lay and kept talking, that sweet endearing little nothings that always melted my heart. I don't remember much about what she said. Hearing her child's voice was so soothing, so comforting and so reassuring. In the coldness of the x-ray room, I held her little hand in mine. Unaware of the fear that possessed me, she told me that she loved me. Tears welled up in my eyes, tears that I fought desperately to disguise from her, but I could feel the warmth of them in that cold room running down my cheeks and dripping off my chin. I tried to wipe the tears from my face without notice for I did not want to upset Kelly. I was aware. I was afraid. I was scared to death. It was a horror that I don't ever want to revisit. That experience was an epiphany showing that all I ever wanted, all I'd ever dreamed for, all my goals, my hopes were wrapped up in this little child with the impish little grin. Nothing, absolutely nothing was worth the loss of my family.

The terror of that experience brought home to me my fear of ever having to bury my wife or my child, and since then it has become my fervent prayer that I will not survive my wife and any of my children. I could not bear to lose any one of them.

These little strangers are a daily reminder of life and of love. These little strangers are the living art of two people in love. A child is the embodiment of a man and woman falling in love and truly becoming one. Children are the true fruition of that commandment that a man and woman become one, for through that child they do. I think, perhaps, if you believe that there is a God as I do, childbirth is the closest we human beings come to the breath of God. It is a miracle we are allowed to participate in. It is a blessing. When we rear a child, the joy of that rearing is given to us as a reward for our partnership with a grateful divinity.

The joy and blessing of childbirth and child rearing, cannot be denied by those whose hearts and minds are open to it. It is generally true that if we do what comes naturally we are more likely than not to be happy. Just as it is natural to eat when we are hungry and drink when we are thirsty, it is natural to find a soul mate, fall in love, consummate that love and bring children into the world. Procreation and renewal are the natural order of things. Satisfaction, contentment and happiness are nature's reward for doing what nature requires of us.

Having and raising children is just a continuation of the love between a man and woman. It is just the next step, the next phase of our love. Love does not stand still. It is constantly changing and developing. It is constantly renewing. Just as children move through phases, crawling before walking, so too does the love between a man and woman. We move from attraction and courtship to passion and then partnership in a great adventure. At each phase love is renewed. It changes. Like a butterfly emerging from its cocoon it is more resplendent, more beautiful. Children are the splendor on the wings of a butterfly; they give us a greater purpose than ourselves. Children are a recommitment of our love, the living parchment upon which we renew our vows, and a reconfirmation of life.

Dear Mother of My Children,

Perhaps it is a good thing that Mother's Day comes around every year to remind the fathers of the gifts that their spouses have brought into their lives... the gift of children. You have given me our children. It was truly a gift from love and of love. It was a gift that was thrice made from a miracle thrice blessed, a gift as divine as love and life itself, gifts as remarkable as they were exciting and moving.

These are the memories that love is built upon. The memory of the love exchanged at conception; the memory of a growing wonderment; the memory of life stirring and pressing against the ear and the hand held to your abdomen; a memory of wondrous and uncontainable expectation; a memory of tender moments shared; a memory of unbearable joy . . .

But motherhood was more than just the creation of children, it was the raising and developing of children . . . the memories of white mice in alarming numbers; parties with excited, joyous and displeased children running hither and yon on little legs; the soccer games; the boy scouts, girl scouts and cub scouts; the fortresses created from empty milk cartons; the orphanage for too many ducks; the unsightliness of art works on walls, created by little hands and feet . . .

What a life you have given us.

Happy Mother's Day

With familiarity all strangers cease to be strangers at some point. They become acquaintances, and sometimes, they become friends, but for these little strangers, we loved them at first sight. The irony is that though strangers from the moment of birth, strangers they have never been. They were in the making long before their mothers and fathers were born. Their parents began to know them when they first met and fell in love. For in these little strangers, we met ourselves. In them we saw our love. They mirrored our courtship, our vows, our passion, our love. They are the aggregate of all who came before, their grandparents, their great-grandparents. They are, after all, in every sense of the word, the "one" their parents had become.

They are the living trophies of our love and of the love that came before. As part of their wedding ceremony, my daughter Erin and her husband Tyrone alternately poured gold and brown sand into a crystal vase, as a symbol of the melding of two lives. That vase with the different colored sand became a keepsake to remind them of their vows to each other. Someday their children will be the reality of their two lives having become one. They will be the incarnation of all their love, their hopes, their vows. Each child will represent all of the both of them; an incomparable keepsake that will endure long after that glass vase had been boxed and forgotten and long after they are gone.

They grow up and we grow up with them and that process is a lot of fun. It is fun getting to know them, and it is difficult at times watching them grow. It is the "sweet sorrow" of parting and the contradiction of life, we want them to grow, but we don't want them to grow away from us.

Dearest Daughter,

Watching your struggles and your relentless pursuit of your dreams is much like watching you take your first steps as a toddler. We watch with fear that every step may bring a stumble, a fall, a bruise, a cut. Every time you seem shaky or your legs begin to wobble we must fight the temptation to run to your support. We know that we must let you walk on your own for only living life can prepare you for life and only living life can result in living life to the fullest. Learning to deal with failure will prepare you for the success that will come your way.

When Kevin was five or six years old, we would occasionally go out on the town together for Men's Night Out. This would usually be on a Friday at the end of my work day.

There came a Friday when we decided to have his mother put him on a bus to take him downtown to meet me. After doing so she was to call me and I was to arrange to be at the bus stop across the street from my office.

I remember how scared I was. What if he got lost? What if he got off at the wrong bus stop? Fear of losing him filled my head, and my heart started beating rapidly and my hands grew sweaty. The phone rang. His mother said that he had been placed on the bus. I tried to time myself. I estimated that it should take about 45 minutes for it to arrive at the bus stop, but to be absolutely safe, I assumed it would take one half hour. I could not work. I could not read the memoranda and documents before me. My mind was seized with the fear that time would pass before I knew it or that I would be distracted and forget to be there at the right time. I paced nervously around the office. I got up from my desk many times for no apparent reason. I walked to nowhere for no good purpose. Mercifully, the time approached and I was early to the bus stop in case the bus was faster than expected. I stood and I paced. Five minutes after my arrival, a city bus approached. As it did I stretched to see if I could see him. I couldn't. I held my breath. Was this the right bus, I thought. Could I have missed the correct bus? It pulled up and stopped. I looked again through the windshield but could not see him. I rushed to the entrance of the bus. Then the bi-fold doors opened with a loud hiss for what seemed like an agonizing moment. There he stood at the top of the stairs looking sheepishly right out at me, sucking the thumb of his left hand, while his right hand played over the remaining fingers. There, under that thumb, was an almost imperceptible grin of triumph. I let out a moan of relief as the anxiety quickly melted away. I gathered him up and hugged him tightly for a long time, much relieved that he was safely in my arms. My eyes filled with tears of pride. My little boy had taken his first adventure into the world by himself and now he was safe in my arms. I walked with him to my office. His little hand was safely in mine and my eyes stared down at him as though I had seen him for the very first time. I was walking on air. It was a proud moment I will never forget. It was an adventure I loathe to repeat, yet one that I knew would be repeated over and over again until my last breath.

It is difficult to explain why that fear-filled, yet prideful moment, stayed etched in my memory. It was such a simple, seemingly unremarkable event. For that time, I was no longer focused on my work, my business and myself. I was concerned only about one thing, the safety of my son. All my mundane worries were trivialized by those anxious minutes. Suddenly, I awoke from the self-absorption of my practice to realize how vulnerable my happiness was, how it had become dependent on the happiness of someone else, a stranger who had entered my life and forever changed it. I do know that the pride I felt was heightened by the anxious moments that preceded his safe arrival. It was so much sweeter. I came to realize that happiness, in part, is knowing that I should be happy. The joy of children is the privilege of loving them above all else and the perspective on life that that love returns to me whenever that perspective is lost.

CHAPTER FIVE

Empty Spaces

Strangers leave empty spaces and lonely places in a father's heart.

A friend once told me that God does not give us children; he lends them to us for a short time. He is right. Yet how many times have young parents heard older people admonish them to enjoy their children while they can? They have been told this so many times that they grow numb to its wisdom. Some would even scream if they heard that admonition repeated one more time. No parent can be reminded enough that their children are only on loan to them, and that they should enjoy them before the period of the loan suddenly ends. They are reminded about this by those who have traveled that road and now suffer the loss. They are called "empty nesters," those who are left only with their memories of the fulfillment that children bring.

Now, when I go back home, you and Kelly will be gone. A home is not a home without all of you in it. Thank God for Erin. She is able to fill many lifetimes with her energy and ebullience and zest for life. She is more delightful than the shimmering reflection bouncing off of a summer pond. It seems that God knew what he was doing when he tacked Erin on as the rear guard. Some thought must have been given to soften the blow to mom and me from an emptying home. A home is fragile when not filled by the taunts and screams, shouts and cries of all of its members. Warm memories still haunt it soothingly.

Kelly was the last of my children to live at home while she pursued her doctoral degree in psychology. In her final academic year as she prepared to take on the defense of her dissertation, everything seemed to move at warp speed. She applied for a position as an associate professor; she was accepted by and contracted with George Fox University; she was flying to Newberg, Oregon to settle into an apartment; she was walking in a graduation ceremony at the Stan Sheriff Center at the University of Hawaii, and she departed for Oregon to commence her first year of teaching. Notwithstanding the time it took for her to graduate and all the admonitions of her pending departure, it still seemed to be a very rude surprise.

Our four-bedroom, three-bath house was empty, but for my wife and me. My life had changed before it seemed that I was aware the change was even approaching. I would no longer hear her at the front door struggling with the keys late at night. She would not appear in the family room, when my wife and I were watching Jay Leno, to report on her day. We would not hear her again announce, "up'um stairs'um" while stretching her arm up toward and pointing to the ceiling to indicate that she was moving up to her room and retiring for the day. Our last to leave had gone. Despite all the warnings, all the fears, all the emotional preparation, her departure was as rude as the discovery of a house ransacked. The strangers that we had taken in so many years ago have gone.

It was difficult even to go into her bedroom.

Unwanted Spaces

Who needs spaces? Where once there was a clutter of dusty books, packages and piles of paper, now there is space on the white Berber carpet of her bedroom. I had not seen that space for so many years. I had forgotten there was carpet there.

The hangers hang from the closet rods pining for the dresses, sweaters and blouses that once they proudly bore. Now the back closet wall is plain to see and there is space everywhere.

In her closet, on her bed and strewn in other places, many orphaned teddy bears and other stuffed toy animals look sad and forlorn. They had been given into pretty little hands many Christmases ago. Now the memories of the joy, the laughter and the hugs they brought are but distant echoes in all those spaces. They once were encircled tightly by little arms, but now those arms have grown as did those legs that took them.

She is gone. The light that lit that room is out. The light that lit our lives every day is away. She has taken it with her. Now that light must shine on many others besides her parents. Now the torch she carries must guide the many young lives who are trying to find their way. Now that light will show the way for many who are still in darkness. Those upon whom that light will shine will be found again. It is her ministry to take that light with her; it is ours to suffer the loss of that light.

Now it is our time to share that light with the world. We are proud to share her; we are sad to share her. Spaces are merely empty remembrances of what was once there. There is emptiness in this room; there is emptiness in our house. It is a proud day that she has gone; it is a sad day that she departed. There is sadness and joy and a lot of spaces in our hearts that have grown accustomed to the charm of little feet and little faces.

When Kevin graduated from law school, I wrote:

My Dear Son,

When we first met, your lap was so tiny I could only pat it with a finger. When you were a toddler and I would pat your lap, my hand would fold around your skinny little legs. Now that you are fully grown my hand hurts when I pat those muscular thighs. Each pat seems to have measured your years and your growth. Each pat on your lap was my assurance to you that I was there and that I would always be by your side as you grew. Each pat meant that I was glad you were there and glad you were with me.

Thank you for having made those years so wonderful. Thank you for creating those occasions so frequently when I would swell with pride beyond what many would deem conceit. I enjoyed every moment. You

*have made me proud, my son, and if indeed it was
sinfully immodest, then I have gone beyond a father's
deserving of any pardon on this recent occasion of your
graduation from law school.*

*Now, son, you must turn your education into skills
sharpened with virtue, hard work, fortitude, patience and
perseverance, and you must sheathe those skills always
with love, sensitivity and compassion. So armed, you
must go forth, slay a dragon, save the village, fall in love
with a fair maiden, raise a family and pass through this
life having made a difference.*

*As for my fair maiden and me, we must look into
the eyes of our grandchildren and see forever.*

Kelly had really enjoyed her undergraduate years, but
she now was preparing for graduation from college. She would
receive her Bachelor of Arts degree from Linfield College. I was
feeling her joy and her sadness at the approaching end of a
very special period of her life, and I was also sad because she
was entering yet another phase of her life that would take her
even farther away from me.

Hi Squeaks,

*I wish I could kiss away the sadness and leave
only the joy, but my powers are mortal and my love
comes from a mortal heart. Yet it seems that God has
given us power to love beyond our mortal bounds. Since
God is love, the power to love is divine. Do not fail to see
the joy through the cloud of sadness. Do not let the*

excitement of the moment be dulled by the sadness that accompanies all joy. With every beginning there is an end. At the end of everything there is a beginning. The key to happiness is the power to embrace the light even in the darkness. After all, you have achieved a college degree with grace, with honors and acclaim. You have honed your skills, increased your knowledge, and laid the basis for true wisdom and enlightenment. You should be proud and excited to put what you have learned to use. When you were born and as you grew up you brightened our lives. There are many, many more lives that now need your light. This is a time to celebrate, to be exuberant, to be festive, to dance and to rejoice. Do not let the shadows you encounter with the beacon of your heart overwhelm you. After all, they are but shadows, and you hold the torch.

As I think back on all these events -- my children's graduation from high school and college, Erin's marriage and so many other changes in their lives, I have come to wonder whether the emotions of those events were more intensely felt by me than by them, for as they experienced the events of their lives, so did I.

CHAPTER SIX

Ducks, White Mice, Birds, Dogs

"In his final hours, I held him close to me, kissing his beak, scratching his neck and holding him against the warmth of my cheeks. As the light in his eyes began to flicker, I pleaded softly to him not to die."

My son Kevin went into the woods close to our house and came back with two Muscovy ducks. What made this a story is that one was male and the other female. What followed was an explosion of dozens of ducklings, for it would seem that these ducks were sex crazed, not to mention that besides the eggs, they produced plenty of fertilizer that burned the lawn and generated complaints from our neighbor. My children loved the ducks; Kevin loved the pugnacity of the original male duck he named Donald; Kelly and Erin loved the ducklings. Donald would sit in waiting for Kevin to come home from school, and when he did, Donald found much sport in provoking Kevin by pouncing on him. Donald was not one to take advantage of surprise; he was too genteel for that. There was always a warning before he pounced; he would hiss and raise the feathers on his back. There would usually be an exchange of taunts between feathered foe and the boy before the physical confrontation. Kevin derived a lot of pleasure in telling of his exploits in beating back the mad duck.

Kelly and Erin would give baths to the ducklings whether they needed baths or not. Afterward, they would dry them off with hair dryers by the fireplace. As they did, the girls would sprawl on the living room carpet propping their chins in their hands and staring with contentment at the ducklings in front of the crackling fire. As I looked on in satisfaction at this sight, the ducks faded into the background and I was looking only at the wonderment in my daughters' faces lit up by the blaze with the reflection of the flames dancing in their eyes. I was grateful to those ducks for bringing so much joy to my children.

Besides the ducks and the white mice, we had dogs, Oscar being our very favorite. He was a cute, affectionate and smart terrier mutt that we adopted from the Humane Society. His preferred mode of demonstrating affection and friendship was to lick a person with his tongue until his tongue was dry; it never happened, however, that his tongue was ever dry. The lickings he gave people left them drenched and in need of a life preserver. His death was, perhaps, our greatest family crisis at that point in time. Now his ashes rest in a little tin container on our bookshelf.

He was replaced by Max, a cute, blond terrier mutt we also adopted from the Humane Society – one month after Oscar died. There was such a void that our search for another dog was needed therapy for all of us. To my dismay, Max later proved to be not very bright. Learning tricks and obedience to simple commands was his greatest deficiency, but he is a loyal, lovable and affectionate dog. Keeping Max clean and free of stink is a challenge because he's shaggy and his hair gets tangled and dirty, and he sheds into everything, including the crevices of the deck. Carol likes him shaggy, so unless I intervene by brandishing the scissors on occasion, he remains difficult to keep clean. When we take him for walks, it's like dragging a stinky shag carpet around the neighborhood. Moments after he gets a bath, he rolls in the grass and dirt as if to mock us. Giving Max a bath is difficult because he pretends to hate water and getting wet. In fact, when the ground is wet from rain Max can be seen tiptoeing over the puddles to get to where he wants to relieve himself. He prefers my wife's attention over mine, and for good reason; I have difficulty forgiving him for being so dumb.

We've also had a parakeet, two lovebirds and a conure named Baby, Snerks, Sneaks and Traddles, respectively.

Traddles was a large green conure that I received as a gift from a cousin who had my father deliver it to me. His beak and his wing span dwarfed those of all my other birds put together. His beak was fearsome, and my children were afraid of him. This gave me the fun of chasing them around the house with Traddles holding onto my arm for dear life while flapping his wings excitedly in the rush up and down the stairs and from room to room. They were delightfully afraid of him. Traddles had the habit of walking up to someone backwards, as if by doing so that person wouldn't see him. That was his way of "sneaking up" on someone. His squawk, however, was so loud that we had to keep him in the garage for the sake of everyone's sanity.

One night we discovered two toads in our garage. They were jumping over each other in a corner, scrambling to make their escape, but they were too clueless to understand how counterproductive that was. Kelly named them Sneaks and Snerks. I liked the names. I thought the sound of those names was as cute as my daughter who named them, so I called our yellow love bird Snerks. Snerks was a very smart and affectionate lovebird. When he died, I wrote the following about him:

Little Yellow Bird
In dedication to Snerks

My little yellow lovebird passed away today. In his final hours, I held him close to me, kissing his beak, scratching his neck and holding him against the warmth of my cheeks. As the light in his eyes began to flicker, I pleaded softly to him not to die.

He was just a little yellow bird, but he always sought my attention and protested when I ventured too far from him. He loved to sit on my shoulders and rub his beak up against my cheek. He took an interest in what I was eating and would beg a piece to taste. When I turned my lips to the right or left away from him, he would tug at my ear trying to turn my lips back to him.

He was just a little yellow bird, but he loved to hide under my shirt. There, warmed by my body, he would fall asleep, and I would forget he was there. In the hot summer days, I could barely stand the heat from his body. Whenever I fell asleep on my back with him on my chest, I would wake up with him staring down at me while standing on my chin.

He was just a little yellow bird, but whenever I began to stir from the covers in the morning or when I came into the room, he would greet me enthusiastically even though I may have broken into his sleep. Most of the time, he would climb all over his cage entreating me to put him on my shoulder. When I did not, he would reproach me by beating his beak against the cover of his cage.

He was just a little yellow bird, but oh how he chirped with glee whenever I placed him on my shoulder. He seemed deliberately gentle when he kissed my soft lips with his hard beak. He would climb up and down my shirt and get into the newspaper I was reading. He liked to bite off pieces of the paper and wad it up in his beak.

He never turned me down when I needed to fill my empty spaces of time with his silly little antics. He would cock his head when listening intently to my clumsy attempts at carrying a musical note. He made a mess on my shirts, but I knew that he was just a little yellow bird.

We buried his little body in a hole my wife had dug on the side of our house. With teary eyes she whispered a prayer over him, but I did not want to tarry over just a little yellow bird.

Now my shirt is clean. My shoulder is without him. I no longer feel his beak on my cheek. I wish I did not miss him so, for he was just a little yellow bird.

Snerks' death had apparently so affected Erin she wept when hearing of it. Snerks had been a member of our family for so long and had been my shoulder companion for years.

She and Tyrone decided that they would replace him with a gift to me of another lovebird. This idea had apparently been hatching in their minds for months when Christmas season of

2006 provided them the opportunity. We happened to be at the mall on other errands when they managed to lead me into the pet store. There were just two hand-raised lovebirds left in the cage, and customers before us had their eyes on one of them. I am sure this caused Erin and Ty a bit of anxiety when the store clerk reached into the cage to remove one of them. Now there was just one left. Erin and Tyrone had invested so much emotion into springing this surprise gift that it became apparent that they were fearful that I would not be satisfied with the remaining lovebird.

I was not quite ready for another pet so soon after Snerks died, and it usually is my practice to observe hand-raised lovebirds in their cage for some time before making a decision on which to adopt. Birds are like people, they have different personalities. Some are more neurotic, some are friendlier, some more playful and some even smarter. I usually need some time to study them, but in this case, there was just one left and it was evident that Erin and Ty were determined to give me a bird to replace Snerks during the holidays. This was to be a heartfelt gift that the both of them had eagerly looked forward to presenting to me. The pressure was on. I had to make a decision then while their anxious eyes were on me.

The two options were clear. If I went about my usual practice of studying the bird, it would take too long and the bird may be taken home by someone else. But most of all Tyrone and Erin would be disappointed. Without other birds in the cage it would be impossible for me to observe the birds' social behavior. No instructive comparisons could be made. If I purchased the remaining bird, it would make my anxious daughter and son-in-law very happy. It was still the holidays, our time for merriment. The choice became clear within seconds as I assessed the situation. I took home a new lovebird.

I named this love bird Sneaks after the other toad that Kelly had named. Sneaks, they said, is a mutation. He is very pretty and has many colors. His beak is dark red. He looks as though he has permanent lipstick on. His eyes are circled by white as though he had indelible mascara. He wears a feather coat with various shades of green and black, but his neck is encircled by thick lei of yellow feathers. His head is black with shades of gray. He was just a baby when we brought him home in a little box. Thanks to Erin and Tyrone, but most of all thanks to them for the love expressed in their planning, conniving and fussing, all leading up to the acquisition of Sneaks.

Sneaks is doing well, and his domination is assured and moving apace. Still a little skittish, in an attempt to get away, he flies off my shoulders and scampers on the carpet to nowhere very quickly. With his wings clipped and my longer legs, of course, he cannot outrun me. I casually stride over to him on the floor deliberately placing my towering figure over him so as to intimidate him. He stops between my legs and stays there for many seconds contemplating the hopelessness of his position. His head barely reaches my ankles. He assumes a submissive position and lowers his shoulders He is practically sitting on his little feet with the feathers of his abdomen covering them and touching the floor. I don't move. I just stand there staring down at him as though staring through the opposite end of a telescope. He finally looks up at me by cocking his little head several times as though wondering what my next move will be. I remain motionless. He continues to cower between my planted feet waiting for my next move as though lightning could strike him very soon. When it sink in that his attempts at flight are futile and that the two-legged, flightless, featherless ogre who keeps him caged will have to be accommodated, I pick him up and gently plant a kiss on his little red beak. I am intoxicated with power.

When we first moved into our second house, just one lot above us there was a large area that had been bulldozed in preparation for further residential development. It was a construction site, but no house yet standing. Some of the streets had been paved and the dirt pads for future houses had been built at various grades, providing level areas for play and the exercise of unbridled imaginations, and dirt ramps, slopes and slides for gleeful children on bicycles. It remained in that condition for years. The construction area and the woods surrounding it became Kevin's playground. He and his friends would ride their bicycles down and over the open spaces, and they loved exploring the surrounding woods. It was a dream; it was a natural playground just yards from our home. I loved watching them race up and down the slopes, jumping over dirt inclines, hiding in trenches and shouting with joy at each other and laughing wildly as they did.

I watched all of this and every event of my children's lives as they were growing up -- the proliferating white mice, the multiplying ducks, the construction area, their entry into kindergarten, high school, college and their graduations -- and I keenly felt sorrow as well as joy at the beginning and end of each phase. I felt sorrow for my children when the duckling phase came to an end. The sheer numbers of mice and ducks forced Carol to find adoptive homes for all their thriving pets. I felt sorrow too when the developer began to build on the construction site where my son had enjoyed so much play. This convenient play ground would soon give way to new houses.

CHAPTER SEVEN

Growing Up

Watching fearfully and guiding gently and wisely was this father's happy burden.

As a child, Kevin was as energetic as any other boy his age, but there were times when for long minutes he would sit quietly and pensively in a corner, on a sofa or out in the yard. He would suck his thumb and appear to be buried in thought. When he would retreat into his thoughts like this, I felt, however briefly, that he left me and I would be fearful. As I watched him alone in his thoughts, I knew he was in a world where I was excluded. It was a place I could not go. Kevin had the ability to leave me in an instant and retreat into this world. I worried that there were demons there that would take my son from me. I wondered what thoughts were going through his mind and what emotions were being felt, but I knew then, even when he was a child, that whatever those thoughts and feelings were, my son was prone to struggling with them and to feeling them intensely.

When a beloved Aunty died, Kevin wrote this loving and beautiful tribute. It was a tribute that said more about Kevin than it did about Aunty.

Aunty O.D. on the day you join us in spirit…
I did not know the last time I kissed your cheek…
That you were planning to leave.
You came here 70 years ago across an unfamiliar sea
Only Buddha at your chest…
Sent to meet a man you did not know…arranged from across the ocean…
Yet you spent your entire life with him…and loved him…
You bore him seven children…raised them with a Chinese, African, Mexican, English and ghetto dialect…in the demographically shifting LA…you stayed in one place despite the prejudices of the other communities who could not stand people who looked like you or each other…
How did you and Uncle carry the family through such drastic changes?
When Uncle passed away I know your heart was torn…
I could see your tears even in your smile…
I would sit and watch you sleep…your tired body…
Waiting to truly rest.
But of everyone you still smiled…
Fed everyone…
Always ate food from many days before while the youth ate the new that you had cooked…
Did they notice this?
If they didn't, why not?
You made everyone smile… even if you were alone…
I would sit with you in the quiet room…
Away from the family…watching a Mandarin movie…

When you could only speak Cantonese…
I concentrated on your cute smile…
How much longer would it remain?
Perhaps, I should have noticed that you were
planning to die…
I did not know that Uncle was calling you…
I hear you calling…"Boy you likee, you likee, no
likee…"
"You take care boy…You take care…"
I know your life was long and hard…but sweet.
I knew it hurt to see your culture swallowed by
America…
I know that you could not identify with the younger
generation…
So I would sit with you in your quiet haven…
Away from it all…
Waiting to rest…
YOU ARE LOVED.
Who will hold the family together now?

When I read this, I was plunged into the grief he was feeling, but I was grateful that he let me into his private thoughts. He is a person of great sensitivity and profound feelings and a good sense of right and wrong. Although smart and extremely talented, Kevin is modest to a fault. As a result, Kevin's good friends sometimes have a stronger belief in his abilities and talent than does Kevin himself. He has a powerful ability to empathize and to be compassionate and to love. He has an open and generous heart. He is a quiet example and a quiet leader for his acquaintances and friends of many ethnicities -- Samoan, Tongan, Chinese, Japanese, Korean, Caucasian, African American. He has fulfilled the prophesy of his Chinese middle name that means a great man who unites different worlds. It is why, I surmise, that so many, including men older than he, and so many of his friends, have told me that they "love him." Kevin has all the makings of true greatness.

He worked as a certified nurse's aide for Aloha Nursing and Rehab Center, a care facility for the elderly. Here he saw and cared for the feeble, the sick, the old and the dying under the most trying circumstances. I wondered whether he could endure it. I knew that I could not have.

I visited there one evening when I went to pick him up from work. As I was coming through the front door, an elderly man startled me by gesticulating wildly, pointing angrily, clenching his fists in a challenging and hostile manner and shouting obscenities loudly at me and anyone else who came through the door. I was startled and briefly unsettled. I was in that state when Kevin came out from another room. Upon seeing him, the elderly man, who had seemed so angry, immediately calmed down, and like a child, took Kevin by his arm, as though thankful for his presence, as though his urgent need, whatever it was, was soothed by him. Kevin smiled at him and held his arm firmly and compassionately and then proceeded to introduce me to this man. This elderly man who had just a second ago seemed so angry and violent became gentle in Kevin's arms. I was enormously moved by my son's compassion. I was very proud of him.

Even after he was no longer employed there, Kevin would visit some of the elderly patients who had become his friends. During those visits he would play his ukulele and sing for them, such was his tenderness and humanity. Kevin often spoke of their personal suffering and even their deaths with sadness, but also with an uncommon kindness tempered with the salve of humor and laughter. Kevin could describe otherwise sad and depressing situations such as Alzheimer's, senility, constipation and death with humor. This ability provided a comic relief for all those concerned, but mostly for himself. It enabled all to better cope with the sadness and sorrow that visited these care homes on a daily basis.

I admire these qualities in him, for the absence of those qualities in me is a discomfiting contrast. Kevin is much like his mother, unselfish and always thoughtful of others. I was and am awed by it. He is so much a better person than I am. Kevin is very different from me. He may never be rich or famous, but he has true and uncommon greatness.

After obtaining his certification to be a nurse's aide, he provided care to others on a private basis, including a stroke victim and a professor with quadriplegia. I became acquainted with them, and without exception they told me that they loved my son, prized his friendship and spoke of him in the dearest and most praiseful terms. They spoke of having observed the humanity, the unselfishness and the compassion that I have long seen in him ever since he was just a little boy.

Such powerful feelings that he has can lead to genius and creativity; they can also lead to despair and depression. I worried about it, and I was relieved that it eventually led to the former. He must continue to exercise his gift of such great talent, not just in the creation of music, but in his writings, because the feelings he has and the challenges he has overcome are shared by millions whose lives can be made better if he does. I was happy that his writings and his songs allowed him to express and to relieve his many deep, pent-up and overflowing emotions.

He must now focus his many talents, his creativity, and his intelligence to support and benefit himself, not so he can become rich, but in order to grow and support his family and improve upon the lives of those he loves and will love.

I think Kevin is deeply affected by the changes around him as seen in the songs he has written. In many of them, there are allusions to the many changes his young heart had to endure, including the tragedies that have plucked many friends from him.

One of his close friends took his own life, and Kevin would visit his grave. When he did, he would play his ukulele, sing and speak to his friend's spirit. After one of those visits with his friend Kawai, he wrote the following:

Brother...
I enjoyed sitting on the hill with you.
Kawai and I sang a song or two...
And I saw the sun set...
Its orange glow... and the gold rays of light...
The hand of God reaching down to pet the earth...
He must have done the same for the others....
This we all hope...
Some have left and some have gone...
One brother shook the soul out of a baby...
The other broke his grandmother's head with a bat...
One shot a taxi driver to death....
One still lives, but may have a bullet lodged in his brain...
Each had no reason but for the substance in their minds...
And the abuse that life took on them.
My other brother was murdered not long after I last saw you...
No one knows why, and I still wrestle with it today.

For none did I cry…for most I had only anger.
How many can we reach…how many will we lose?

For I got angry at the people of this land…
Of this country…and I hated them all…
Because their minds were full of mess…
Messy, messy, waste…living and breathing it…
I thought…

But you taught me to be concerned…you knew I loved
all…For you thought inside…who could ever love
you…and I did…
Brother, you said you would stand by my side…
You taught me to let my barriers go…
To free my soul…because you felt I could free others…
But I have found that I am still chained…
And I have no key to offer another…
And so my brother, I am lost as you were…
Alone as well…
I am losing my concern for so many….
I am going back into myself…
Where I know myself best…
Where I can just be…
And have no answer.

How many have I lost? So many since I have come and
gone…
It is good that others come into my heart when others
leave.

Dear Brother, it was good to see you…
Kawai and I sat quietly among the rest…
Playing a tune for you…

I enjoyed sitting beside you on the way.
Just the two of us in the dark.
I felt safe as you steered my car across that hateful new sliver of gray
Through your beloved mountains.
I felt proud as I walked with you through the theater…
To watch an offering or two from Hollywood.
I felt you hurting.
Your heart was pulling the rest of you back inside
Where mere words could not follow.
Yet I am often awed by this boy of mine
Who has grown into a man of strong feelings.
Feelings that hover so fragilely between love and hate, sympathy and anger.
I love you for how much you care.
I've seen you as a cuddly, warm doughboy, and the funniest of clowns.
And I've watched you plunge into despair for the loss of your brother.
But more than these…
I saw a man of great strength who is destined to be an anchor for others.
Don't despair for long, son.
No one has the answer.
(Many of us don't even know the question.)
I am watching you grow, knowing that without pain there is no growth.
You are my hope for the world.

But this stone with your name next to where I sit…
Is not the same…it is cold…
And I miss your warm heart.

In this writing in which Kevin mourns the loss of his friend, he goes in and out of anger and flirts with despair. He disguises his own feelings by the feelings of his friend. It is not easy to know who he is talking about and whose feelings he is referring to, but it is clear that as he speaks about his good friend, he merges identities. This device allows him to detach himself from his own feelings, and by doing so, he seems enabled to freely express himself. He is able to examine his feelings outside of himself as though he were able to put his feelings on the examining room table and inspect them with objectivity. He is often speaking of himself, though he appears to be speaking of his friend. He feels free to merge identities because they were kindred spirits, because they shared the roller coaster of feelings that were confusing and overwhelming for them at a crucial time in their development.

Educating independent thought requires provoking thought by raising unsolvable questions; in young, immature minds this can be dangerous. This writing seems to mark a point in time after Kevin had reached the shore by gaining intuition into his own inner struggle. He describes it as "feelings that hover so fragilely between love and hate, sympathy and anger." The sharing of their feelings enabled both of them to cope. His friend had lent him strength, but the irony is that his friend succumbed, and it is Kevin that reached the shore, and there is a sense that Kevin feels a little guilt because he is the survivor. Yet there seems to be a recognition that he, in part through the help of his friend, has learned to cope with the seeming hopelessness of life's many questions. By successfully bridging the chasm, he is strengthened and he realizes that he can help others do the same. He says, for example, "I see a man of great strength who is destined to be an anchor for others."

The graveyard setting and the senseless deaths of friends seem to mirror the despair this confusion of mind plunged them into, but the "gold rays of light" and "the hand of God reaching down to pet the earth" contrast eerily with the coming darkness and gloom of the cemetery. It seems to awaken the hope and exhilaration that comes from the acceptance that "no one has the answer." From this "pain" Kevin has become stronger. From this, he has become "a man of great strength." When Kevin was an infant, he was chubby and healthy and rounded at every point, and we delighted in calling him our (Pillsbury) dough boy. Kevin is the "doughboy" he is referring to in this writing.

As I have done throughout his life, I shared his heartache and his sadness almost as though they were my own, but I don't think Kevin knew that I shadowed him emotionally as he traveled this difficult path. I am happy that he has safely crossed this part of life. It was a chasm of life that most young people are faced with crossing. It was not an uncommon challenge, but Kevin's feelings about things, about people he cared for and about life, ran uncommonly deep.

In the education of young people, they are taught specific academic courses, each supplying only a piece of a puzzle. Each piece is fraught with seemingly insoluble questions that may disturb young and as yet unripe minds. This may continue until life's experiences catch up with them and enable them to see the entire picture. It is a time that is worrisome to a father in love with his son.

As one grows older, it is wisdom nurtured by experience and knowledge that reins in the excesses of thought and prevents it from turning into harmful behavior. As we grow wiser we grow to accept that answers are few and insignificant in the universe of questions. Wisdom is fully and truly appreciating that we do not know and that we may never know. It is wisdom, therefore, that deters arrogance and extreme thought, for it mercifully robs us of our conceit. We are here to struggle with the unknowable; it is the gauntlet life throws at our feet. We can stand on a hilltop, raise our fists and rail against the stars and break, or we can learn to accept that we are the stars. We are what we rail against.

In the end, I could only look at Kevin from a distance, although I longed to be at his side to protect him whenever he retreated into his mental and emotional struggles. He had to take this trip by himself in order to become wiser, to grow and to mature. As he himself said, "knowing that without pain there is no growth." It is the damnable frustration of fathers to suffer their earthly limitations to help their sons and daughters. All I could do was to love him and to hope that it would be a safe trip.

Some of his songs touch upon the many cultural and environmental changes he has to contend with. "Simple Island People" bemoans changes in the environment affecting the simplicity of island people, such as the encroachment of urbanization on the natural forest behind our house and the loss of that vacant construction area he and his neighborhood friends enjoyed so much. "Overload on Automation" is a humorous protest against the intrusion of a complex world into a simpler island lifestyle, one that Kevin enjoyed so much and loved as a child. "Kupa'aina" has a similar theme that mourns the loss that change brings. Some of his songs speak of love, and the joy as well as the heartache of young romance. While each experience is unique to Kevin, the themes are common.

His songs are about his actual experiences as he grew up and about his feelings as he coped with the changes. As a worried observer of his life, I was familiar from afar with some of his youthful emotions even before he wrote and sang of them, and so his songs allowed me to revisit old memories of watching him struggle with the inner demons, the challenges of growing up, the formation of his thinking mind and relationships, even as far back as when he used to pensively suck his thumb, alone and lost in his thoughts and emotions.

Perhaps, the most meaningful gift I ever made to any of my children was the Kamaka ukulele I bought for Kevin before he went off to his junior year at the University of Oregon. Up to that time he had not seriously played the ukulele very much. I also got him a hard case for his ukulele, music sheets and chord charts to assist him in learning to play it. At a younger age, Kevin had always been interested in music. He collected a lot of audio tapes, many of which I bought for him. I never expected, however, how well he would learn to play the ukulele to accompany his singing. When he returned after the first year he was playing it well, and eventually, he sang as he played, developing a beautiful voice and a uniquely personal and exciting way of interpreting and rendering songs, even those written by others.

Much later, it became apparent to me that he was becoming interested in the guitar. I planned to buy him one. I was really excited about surprising him with such a gift. One day, despite the usual rigors of my schedule, I broke away from my work to go to Island Music on the second floor of Ward Warehouse. It was sometime around the lunch hour. As I approached the store I was surprised to see that Kevin was inside playing and fiddling with some of the guitars on display. What a happy coincidence!. For a long while, I stood outside to watch him. As I gazed through the large storefront window, I did not see Kevin as he really was -- a young college student; I saw a little boy looking longingly at a guitar. It was thrilling to me just to savor that moment. I knew that he could not at that time afford a guitar, but I could, and I wanted so much to get it for him. I finally entered to announce my presence, and before leaving, I bought him a Baby Taylor guitar. I was so happy that it worked out the way it did, and it was so satisfying to get it for him, more satisfying, perhaps, than any gift I had ever made to him except for the Kamaka. For that moment, I felt like a dad again. I felt as though I had been magically given that moment to satisfy my little boy's longing. I still carry that memory with me. It still thrills me when I think about it, when I saw him looking so longingly at some of those guitars. To this day, I don't think he knows why or how it was that his father appeared at that store at that precise time.

As it turns out, the purchases I made contributed, in some small way, to the discovery of his musical talent. He became a songwriter, a musician, a performer, an artist and a producer. So much of the sensitivity and emotions I saw in him as he was growing up, even when he was just a little boy quietly sucking his thumb, and when he ran off to a strange land chasing after a Japanese girl, were being expressed and channeled through his songs and his voice. He had a unique, creative and beautiful way of interpreting and delivering his songs. I was happy that he had been given this talent. It is a wonderful way for him to express and vent the emotions that well up in him at times, emotions that seem pent-up and in need for release. The uncommon depth and breadth of his feelings are the source of his inspiration.

My hope is that he will not just continue to write and compose songs, but that he will continue to write creatively, to inspire and move and touch the hearts of many. For while we think we suffer and feel in silence by ourselves, we are all feeling and suffering together in a family of human beings. Kevin's writings and songs (and those of Tyrone and Erin) have the capacity to lift the spirits of many and help them to cross their personal chasms of life. It is a powerful talent that belongs not just to Kevin, but to those whose lives would be lifted by it.

I certainly was not an exception, for I too had to cross my deep, personal chasms, and I had to struggle with bewildering feelings and emotions. If I had not, I would not have been able to empathize with Kevin as he grew up. As we live our lives with all their bumps and warts, we develop a keen ability to empathize with our fellow human beings and we are better able to meet the challenges of fatherhood. What then happens to those who are not allowed to suffer?

Although my daughters are grown and out of the house like Kevin, they are never far from my thoughts. With every bit of news from them I strived to visualize the lives they were living. My knowledge of them empowered me to fill in the spaces that were left unreported. Ever since they left our home it has become my pastime.

Dear Big Eyes,

This morning Mom briefed me, as she usually does, on your telephone conversation yesterday. She did so in her inimitable style, reading from her notes as a good journalist does.

Mom reported that you told her that you took a walk to the video store, and that during your walk you tried listening for God. Along your way, on a number of occasions, you saw some trash blowing in the breeze. A you heard in your head was a voice saying "Pick up the trash." So you did. You picked up the trash.

After chuckling over it, I thought what a wonderful story. It told me a lot about you. It told me of your spiritual side, your love for God and your search for guidance. That you actually began picking up trash speaks volumes about your sweet nature. Not wanting to possibly miss out on the message, you actually stooped to pick it up.

It revealed your inquiring side; your search for answers is as old as man is old. It begins when you find yourself staring longingly into the infinite star-twinkling heavens and when you are cowed by the awesome power of waves crashing on a rocky shore, relentlessly carving the earth.

I am not as religious as you are. You and Tyrone have been gifted with faith. When they say that faith is a gift, believe it. It is.

I believe, however, that all men are spiritual. From the time they are infants looking curiously through their new eyes into their new world, they are searching. It is a quest as endless as time, a search that never ends. Many believe they are searching for meaning, but I believe that there is meaning in the search, that is, that it is the struggle itself that has meaning. It is when we are on a search for meaning that we become meaningful. On your little walk to the video store, you picked up trash. Although you believed that you never heard a message, you picked up trash. On that path that you travelled, there was one less MacDonald's box, one less candy wrapper, and one less crumpled napkin to despoil the land, to offend another person passing that way. As you read *this, maybe you're thinking what you did was so insignificant, so small. Because you walked that way on that day at that time, the path was so much cleaner, that much more pleasant for anyone who followed.*

I don't think that God shouts in our ear when he delivers a message. I don't think he writes in bold letters in the sky. I think we can hear Him when we listen. Since God is love, we must listen with love. If you want to receive digital messages, you can't do it with an analog receiver. God speaks in the tongue of love. He wrote his messages to me through the miracle of childbirth, in the beauty of motherhood, in the cherubic faces of infants and the mischief of children, in the image of Channing and the prettiness of Italia, in the guava forest behind our home, and the grandeur of the Koolaus, in the freshness of morning air on a country road, and yes, even in the affection of a little yellow bird. When I jog around Ahuimanu Park, I listen for the playful yelps of little children. They remind me of listening to you, Kelly and Kevin, feeding on your mother's milk. To me it is like music.

I believe that these are the messages of God. It comes directly from Him, unspoiled by the frailty of man. You are right, sweetheart, His messages are there all around us. Maybe, that is why part of a loving nature is listening with our hearts.

I love you.

Erin was moved to tears when she came to realize that life was inevitably drawing her away from close and dear friends. Flying away to college, many farewells to friends and family and even new-found romantic interests made her resentful of the changing of long-cherished relationships. I remember many of her tearful goodbyes to her good friend, Tisha. Those farewells grew even more poignant as they both pursued relationships with men in their lives, as though to do so would somehow diminish the love between them. I felt as though I were a third person in their relationship because both Erin and Tisha were so vociferous even when they whispered, because much of their intimate conversations occurred in our home, and because their relationship was so transparent. As many do with things they cherish, they generously shared their relationship with their friends. Their friendship was not exclusive. Because of their generosity of spirit, it could not but be inclusive. Friends were sometimes drawn into the drama life's changes pressed upon their friendship.

There was a time when Erin and Tisha were exchanging thoughts about a difficult decision that Tisha was apparently having so much pain in making. Their conversation was occurring in Erin's room. Erin's room is on the second floor, like a loft in that part of a common wall opened up into the living room. It was obvious even to minimally perceptive people that there was no wall affording any privacy to conversations spoken in that bedroom, even if spoken at a normal volume. Their words would tumble down into the living room and reverberate around the house. This never seemed to bother Erin and Tisha who always spoke to each other at high volume; it was like an open invitation for others to turn on and tune in. It was as though they were born with megaphones built into their voice boxes. Anyone sitting in the living room became an unwitting participant in their most private chats. As it happened, I was in the living room at the time, and since I did not choose to inconvenience myself in my own home by stuffing wax into my ears, I became a reluctant participant. Very soon after listening to this secret conversation, publicly broadcast as just described, it became clear to me that Tisha had allowed her emotions to cloud what was otherwise a very simple thought process. She injected much confusion into her thinking by hopelessly intermingling totally unrelated issues. Armed with this observation, I felt compelled (as I usually am, when my analytical mind enables me to clearly see the way to solving a problem) to rescue her from the confusion that was causing her so much pain. When Tisha was in the bedroom by herself, I came to the doorway to offer her my thoughts. With a few pointed remarks and probing questions, I saw the light of recognition appear on her face. My brief observations seemed to have lifted the cloud that had concealed the solution for so long. A huge smile appeared and her suffering seemed to melt away. The relief was instantaneous.

It was reported to me that Tisha, always a devout Christian, believed that to relieve her of her suffering, God spoke through me. If this is so, I am glad to have been His instrument. I think of it with greater humor, however: God spoke through me because He had no alternative; Erin and Tisha were so loud they disturbed heaven and upset the angels; He spoke to her through me in a desperate attempt to purchase some peace and quiet in heaven.

With each of their struggles they learn to cope with the often sad, inexorable march of time. It just seems to me that I was coping with them in lock-step at every stage. Because I had this ability to see problems before they occurred and to see the issues presented with clarity, I anticipated the phases of their lives and I felt or suffered the emotions of each phase long before they happened. Through them, I was coping with life's changes, the joys and sadness, all over again.

Kelly was perplexed and saddened by her graduation from Linfield College. Like so many other young people who graduate from college, there is much confusion. There is much sadness as well as joy. They can no longer hope to see their friends as they did every day when going to classes or college social events. The morning after receiving that degree, they wake up to a world in which they do not have to take courses, carry books from class to class, attend lectures and complete assignments. From kindergarten through college their lives had been scheduled by others with courses, activities and educational pursuits. Charting their lives for the first time by themselves brings bewilderment, uncertainty and confusion. Kelly was not spared this. I was not spared any of this, for as their father I was with them at their side the whole time like an observer in the shadows watching them cope with the difficulties of change. I was, however, not a disinterested observer; I felt their sadness, their joy, their highs and their lows. Each change signaled a change in my life. As they had to cope with change, so did I have to cope with their changing. It was as though I was growing up all over again.

From birth, it's inherent in our nature to always be dissatisfied with current circumstances. When we are children, we cannot wait to be adults; when we are adults, we wish we had our youth back. When we have curly hair that others would kill for, we want straight hair. Our complexion seems never to be perfect enough, and our friends have flaws. When we have enough money, we want more. When we have all the food we need, it is just not prepared well enough. When rain replenishes our reservoirs, sates the thirst of our gardens, washes our trees and streets and cleans the air, it is too much and comes at an inconvenient time. It is our challenge in this life to find moments of greater happiness by taking a breather from so many unwarranted wants, to step back and be satisfied with the gifts we have. It just seems that life was designed to frustrate our constant search for more perfect happiness. So it is true of this dad.

When I should be happy with the good health of my children, I wonder if they will be safe tomorrow. When they have accomplished so much, I worry what the future holds for their dreams. As they grow up I want them to find good spouses and have healthy and happy families. When they move in that direction, I am anxious they may misstep. When they grow up I wish they were small again. When they become independent, I wish they were back in my arms. When they become responsible for their own lives, I wish they were always close to me.

Months after graduating, Kelly, like most graduates from college, went through a period of confusion and sadness. She was lost and she was trying to find her way. For a time, she believed that God was calling her to go on a spiritual mission to Japan, so she directed her mind and her efforts toward that goal. She set her heart on it and prayed for guidance.

I had many talks with her during this seemingly aimless period of her life. Some were very difficult, tearful and painful. I urged her to question her supposition that God wanted her to go on a mission to Japan.

I tried to gently nudge her toward a suitable goal, one that would fulfill her desires and make her happy. I tried to do it by helping her to think clearly, by helping her to focus and by helping her to lift the fog and confusion of emotion. I told her that I did not believe that God whispered or shouted his intentions in a person's ear or wrote messages in the sky. I believed that God gave each of us a compass to find our own way. To use the gift of that compass, I thought, was the best way to love Him who gave it to her. She should listen to her heart, and that is where she will hear His intentions for her. I told her that I believed that His messages may be written in the gifts He has given her; that it may be read in the strengths and weaknesses He has given each of us that make us so different from each other. It made sense that He would provide each of us with the right equipment and provisions to complete the journey He wants us to take. If He wanted us to swim an ocean or climb a mountain, He would give us the strength and stamina to do it and the passion and heart to sustain it. To know Him and to know what He wants, we start by knowing ourselves.

Kelly's primary strength is her incredible intelligence. She is smarter than all of us in the family. Her brother used to complain that she was able to get excellent grades despite her sleeping in class. Excellent grades and high scores and academic honors seemed to come easy for her. She was a National Honor Society scholar and she graduated *magna cum laude* from high school. There were many instances as she grew up in which she would astound me with her understanding of things complex for her age. Her scores on her college entrance exams were very high; she even wanted to take the exam again to improve upon her score. She was designated a "Linfield Scholar" when she was accepted to that college. She received superlative scores when she took the examinations for graduate studies, and her credentials were described by administrators of the graduate schools as "very impressive." She had always excelled in academia, and since that was the strength God gave her, that is where she came to concentrate her quest.

There was a time in her undergraduate life when Kelly felt that she should be a teacher, but she seemed to have given up on that idea after she had had an unpleasant experience teaching children. To her this seemed to conflict with her desire to help young people. This experience distracted her from a teaching career. As we continued to discuss this, I suggested that it may not have been teaching that was problematic, but rather the grade level she had taught.

There was one thing that was very clear in her mind. She wanted to help young people. I suggested that she could still help young people, maybe not when they were still children, but rather when they were college level. There must be so many college students who would thirst for her guidance and her example. As a professor she could make a difference in the lives of hundreds of our country's young people. Helping young college-age students agreed with her need, spiritual and emotional, to help young people.

The college course she enjoyed most was psychology, but since her analytical and communication skills were exceptional, we also considered law as a possible area of teaching; perhaps she could become a law professor. We went to the William Richardson Law Library at the University of Hawaii where I acquainted her with the law as a course of study with what the practice of law was like and with legal jurisprudence. She decided that she was still partial to psychology. So she focused on that which God apparently had given her a capacity to enjoy.

That is the direction she finally decided on. She would excel in academia, where she always excelled,   teaching college psychology, where her interest and passion lay, in keeping with her long-held desire to help young people. She would become a professor.

It seemed that once she read His messages in her heart, where they always had been, God sent signs of His approval. Her scores and credentials were so high that she was readily accepted into graduate studies in psychology, not just as a student, but as a graduate assistant. In addition, her tuition was waived. Her sponsoring professor had nothing but praise for her and proclaimed that she was the smartest and best student he had ever sponsored for a doctoral degree. Moreover, Kelly was enjoying herself and never looked back at her decision to pursue a college teaching career with a Ph. D. in Psychology.

Through every step of the way I watched her joy as each step confirmed to her that she had made the right choice. I attended and listened to her presentation of her dissertation, and witnessed the awarding of her master's degree. When she defended her thesis, I was there too to observe her performance before good and reputable professors. The little, pretty infant with the impish grin and shock of black hair was impressing these professors, and as she did so, I thought to myself, "Look here. I'm her father." At each step I was so very proud of her. Finally, she walked through the Stan Sheriff Arena wearing her Ph. D. regalia, hood and leis and a soaring smile of immense satisfaction and triumph. When she later applied for a faculty position at a few universities around the country, it became evident that she was considered by them to be the perfect candidate for a teaching position. When she finally accepted a position, it was on a beautiful and supportive campus in a state that she loved. She is today a doctor of psychology and a professor at a small private university with a spiritual and academic mission. It was all that she had hoped for.

Her enjoyment of academia, her uncommon intelligence, her enjoyment of her subject and her desire to help young people were the indicators that converged to direct her to her calling as a university professor. After a period of difficulty, she had not just found her way; she had done it with confidence and excellence. I am so very proud of her.

Kelly is also a very gifted writer and dancer. She has choreographed some of her own dances, and she brings grace and beauty into any room she dances in. As she moves, there is exceptional beauty and grace in her hands and face, and she has used these blessings in signing for the deaf. She has used signing as a mode of personal expression, and through signing she has empowered others to overcome their disability and to more easily join the hearing world. I hope that she will continue to improve on these talents and one day she will dance for her suitors, dance at her wedding and dance for her own children.

As we go through life, parents store up a lot of knowledge and wisdom, the kind of wisdom that like all secrets seems to clamor to be revealed. This may be one reason why teaching as a profession is so satisfying. Children are like precious clay that we mold to meet the likely challenges ahead of them. For each teacher, their student is a work of art, a vessel they pour their talent, effort and love into, like painting on a canvas. Each student is a work of love for them, of dedication and affectionate care. Teachers shape the very face of the future.

This too may be the reason why parenting is so satisfying, for parenting is teaching and more. These children are the canvas for parents to work their craft, to be involved in a direct way, the future of our country and of the world. If children are the canvas, then love is our medium of expression, like paint is to an artist. It is vital work. It is important work. It is essential. Children are the very expression of their parents. We fill our need to make an enduring statement by crafting our children. By shaping them with our love, care and guidance, we craft the future. Children are our truest legacy.

Egyptian pharaohs erected palaces and pyramids to mark their reign. Kings built castles and conquered territory to preserve their kingdom. Presidents establish libraries as a memorial to their legacy. The most enduring and most important legacy of all does not cost the lives of slaves, the blood of men and billions of misdirected dollars. It is a legacy that we can all leave behind. It is not dependent upon the station in life we are born into or the whim of a fickle electorate. The most enduring and important legacy is our children. The price of children is love; the remuneration is love. The currency for raising a family is love.

Inevitably, children grow up to struggle with matters of the heart, and with sons, "the enigma that is woman." My son was in a relationship with a young lady on campus. As he wrote to me about it, I sensed the many uncertainties and conflicts that he was living through.

Hi Son,

Throughout life you meet people you like and those you do not. As you go through life and mature you sharpen your senses. They become keener. Your values set in and you have formed your own radar, so to speak. This radar protects you from danger and it eases you with caution into relationships. This radar is working even as you choose your friends and those with whom you wish to spend more time. You find your own circle where you spend most of your finite time and energy. A person can be defined by the company he keeps, by the friends he hangs out with, by the things he enjoys. Over time thi. radar usually works well in matters of the heart. It cannot be logically defined, analyzed nor intellectually plumbed. It is based on your lifetime of living, constantly reassessing, building, tearing down and building up of relationships, learning what irks you and what gives you pleasure. It cannot be intellectualized. It is like trying to understand why you prefer apples to pears or why another prefers pears to apples.

When finding a good companion or a lifetime mate, there are risks, but your radar plays a greater role in that search than your higher senses. When I met your mother my radar told me that this was the one. It was a scary risk. I trusted my radar more than my higher cognitive functions. In my case, I am damn glad I did. Lif without your mother is inconceivable to me. I cannot bea. to even think of it.

Making a checklist of good and bad does not work It may even harm the process.

Your radar looks out for subtle things, many imperceptible. Does she melt when she sees a beautiful infant? Does she marvel at a flawless rose? Does she return a furtive glance? Does she go on excitedly about the loyalty and the cuteness of a dog? Does she love an respect her parents? Would she run to the side of a friend in need? Does she dislike things that you like? When she laughs at a joke, do you find the joke humorous? Does she like most of the things that you do? Is her reaction to the beauty of the setting sun genuinely one of awe and inspiration? Does she honestly ooooo and ahhh at things soft, cuddly, cute, lovable...? Does *she disappear into her thoughts when standing before the powerful ocean? Does she wonder about the ends of the universe? Is she smart and witty? Does she muse at the meaning of life? Is she perplexed about nature's surprises, and does she express pleasure in thinking on it? Is she reflective about life's ceaseless questions? How does she handle them?*

All this and more your radar processes faster than you can think them. Usually, the radar lets you know that you are attracted to the object on the screen, then that you are very attracted, then that you have deep feelings for the object, then that you want to spend a lot more time with it. The longer it is on the screen, the easier it is to identify. To extend this ridiculous metaphor, the longer it is on the screen the more certain you will be before you send out your heat-seeking missiles.

In conclusion, my son, it is better that there are objects on the screen than that there are none. Remember this......your radar at the age of 25 with all the traits I know you have is better than most and certainly better than mine when I courted your mother.

I love you son. With that, I leave you in your happy conundrum.

Parents traveled down many of the same paths their children are only now beginning to take. We know it. We've been there; we skinned our knees and jammed our toes on the bumps and turns on the highway of life. We know where the potholes are, the curves, the bumps, the many hazards of the road. We can and do try to provide them with a road map highlighting all the dangers that are there. Our fear from their first baby steps carries on through their lives and all the steps they take thereafter. We reason that it is ridiculous that they should skin their knees on the same bumps when we can forewarn them. There is so much logic to that, but once they take the stage themselves, our words are often not heard above the noise of life.

Kevin fell in love with a very pretty girl from Japan. It was his first romantic relationship that I knew of.

I viewed the videotapes of the both of them. I was moved. I was moved, I guess, because this was my son demonstrating so much love for another, so much passion, so much feeling. I was moved, I guess, because this was Kevin at his most sensitive, very sincerest self. He was so profoundly vulnerable, yet so wildly happy. He was at once such a big man and such a little boy, and when this big man laughed and played, poked fun and kissed, swelled and soared, in all his giddiness he was that little boy who frolicked in the mountain streams and rode his bicycle in the construction sites that replaced the guava trees and native ferns he used to trek through. This was the college student and the elementary school boy who delivered papers in the neighborhood. This was the little boy I remembered now wrapped in the 230-pound body of a man. I felt again the joy of his first carousel ride, his exhilaration down Thunder Mountain, his glee on a horseback ride. I saw and felt it all in this videotape of his first infatuation.

After graduation, she went back to Japan. He followed her there, and when he did, so did I. My spirit went with him, with trepidation, to this foreign country, where now as a young college graduate, he followed his heart. I knew even before he went that he would be confronted with many difficulties, and I even sensed what those difficulties would be. I yearned for every bit of news coming from him. It was a growing experience for him as he struggled to support himself in a foreign country without a work visa and at the same time struggled with the direction this love affair was going to take him. It was a time of great emotional challenges for him. It was a time of great growth and maturity.

At times, the hardships he had to endure, briefly declined into cynicism about life and about his host country, not unlike most young people growing up trying to make sense of life's muddle.

The Japanese will not shout with joy at your arrival. You must earn their respect and affection, one at a time. This is true whether you are in Japan or in the good old USA. We know that most Japanese are warm and friendly people. They are good people. ...The unsmiling masks that they wear on the subway, in their commute, while rushing from place to place on the streets conceal their true nature. This is true in all subways and cities in the world. Do not mistake the masks for their hearts and minds.

Through all the difficulties of his experiences in Japan, Kevin seemed to be slowly finding his way through life. He called from Japan to announce that when he returned, he was going to law school. His struggles in Japan had apparently taught him that life's challenges could better be met and overcome with a professional education. His experiences there steeled his resolve and made him determined. He had never before indicated that he was interested in law school. I had never encouraged him to become an attorney. I was very pleased at this decision.

I never deliberately encouraged my children to take any direction toward a specific career. I knew that we all had to find our own way. I tried to focus on their happiness and not any particular career direction. My thought was that whatever career or profession they chose, if it led to their happiness, I should be satisfied. What I usually tried to do, however, was to assist them in thinking their way through the process. I tried to bring focus and clarity to their working out their many questions. Kevin's experiences with the hardships in Japan, however, seemed to be the catalyst that compelled him toward an education in the law.

When he returned home, he immediately applied for admission and was admitted into law school. I felt I could now help my son to do well in law school.

Son,

Keep in mind the following as you go through law school:

Rule 1. Understand to remember. Do not remember to understand.

Rule 2. In the law, there are very little right and wrong answers. There are answers that are better than others.

A better answer is one that is better reasoned, better supported and more persuasive.

Rule 3. If you are not able to explain your answer so that a lay person may understand it, then you do not understand it yourself.

Rule 4. Keep a mental picture of the forest while you examine the leaves and the limbs of the trees.

Rule 5. If you must brief a case, brief it to help you to understand the case, not to substitute for your truly knowing and understanding the case.

Rule 6. Read your cases actively, not passively. Listen to your professor actively, not passively.

Rule 7. Law school should not be teaching the law as much as teaching you to think critically.

Rule 8. Improve your reading and writing skills. Improve your vocabulary.

Rule 9. Begin your reading and your studying the moment you hear the start gun go off so that you will not be rushed in the end. Thoughts and ideas need to be mulled over, tested, examined and chewed on. This takes time. Since memorization is not that important, cramming won't help.

When he was admitted to law school, he took out a large apartment right on campus at my insistence, because the surrounding neighborhood was reported to be crime ridden. I stayed with him for awhile helping him to prepare for his first year, and with the help of cousins living nearby, outfitted his kitchen with utensils, food and supplies. We were able to scavenge around and acquire some needed furniture for his living room and bedroom. It was a privileged time for me to be able to be with him at the beginning of a very important semester, the infamous first year of law school. When my stay was over, I was sad to leave him to begin his first year, but when I left I was very, very proud of his undertaking such a difficult course. Up to that point he was still living at home and I could pretend that he was just a child, but when I left him alone on that law school campus, I had to accept that my son was now an independent adult. It was difficult for me to get back into my car by myself and wave goodbye to him as I drove off.

We are like directors and producers of a play, after tireless instruction to our actors, the time comes when we must set them on the stage to be on their own and without us. We must turn on the lights and raise the curtains. We sit in the back galleries and nervously watch the play unfold, all the while holding our breaths in fretful silence. At times the urge to shout at the stage from the galleries is irresistible. We know that if we give in to such urges, the performers will stop, the lights will go on and everyone on the stage and in the audience will look at us with angry eyes for disturbing the flow of the play. Chastened, we shrink back into our seats as the lights dim again and the play resumes. We are afraid that if we give in to such urges, the performers may merely hesitate in mid-sentence, and in a blink of an eye the action would resume just as though nothing had intruded, just as though nothing had been said, just as though our words were no longer heeded. Once the play is afoot it is very difficult to make adjustments.

We are all born to love and to be loved. Although we cannot explain it, it is so, and it is so even if we do not admit it. The beauty of love is that we have the power to generate more love and as much love as we want for others and for ourselves. The source of its creation and the power to receive and give it are within us. We are able to manufacture love almost at our whim. We can do so whenever, wherever, for as much and for as long as we want.

Despite the power of it, it has always been curious to me that the word love is given no more important status than any other word in a dictionary. Lexicographers have defined love as: "deep affection and fondness", "sexual relation", "sexual passion", "delight in", "greatly admire", "greatly cherish", "greatly enjoy". All such definitions fall so miserably short of what we have come to feel as love.

Even without an adequate definition, love exists. Of that, there can be no denial. Though love defies description, it is just as sweet. It is just as pleasurable, just as rejuvenating, exhilarating, healing, exciting and wonderful. It is just as real.

Dear Daughter,

A friend who was a corrosion control expert once explained to me what rust was. He said that when natural iron ore is taken from the ground it is amorphous, shapeless and of little use. We submit that iron ore to a great amount of energy, intense heat, and melt the ore into molten steel. We then form that steel into girders of various shapes and sizes. These girders are then shipped around the world to be used in thousands of structures. He said that rust is the steel wanting to return back to the earth, wanting to become iron ore again. Electro-chemical reaction unbinds the energy that had kept the steel from returning to iron ore.

I never forgot that story from my good friend. I wondered how that analogy could be applied to us and what instruction could be derived from it. My thought is that we come from materials that our mothers consumed. These are mineral, vitamins, proteins and other nutritional ingredients from vegetables, milk and meat products consumed by our mothers during gestation. All of these come from the earth, like the iron ore. They are all raw ingredients. Your mother made sure she took good care of herself when she was pregnant, always eating the right things, taking fluoride and calcium to strengthen your teeth and bones, and taking the nutritional supplements recommended by her doctor whom she saw as frequently as needed. She took care not to drink alcohol or subject herself to too much smoke. She was never more lovely, radiant and beautiful than when she was pregnant with each of you.

I have often wondered, however, what the energy was that formed these materials into living, breathing infants. In the case of the iron ore it was energy in the form of thousands of degrees of heat. A mother's body does not have such a furnace. I wondered what that energy is that takes the material she eats and shapes our children.

I have over the years surmised that it is love. They say that love moves mountains. I truly believe that it does. It is a form of energy that science has yet to recognize. We know that science has not yet discovered all forms of energy in the universe, and on occasion science discovers more, such as black energy, neutrinos etc. Maybe love is one form of energy that science has overlooked. It would not be the first time that energy in a form not detectable to human senses remained undiscovered for a long time. Science believes that the universe, including Earth, came into existence from an astronomical explosion, a Big Bang. The energy from that explosion took the form of the stars, asteroids and planets. Everything, it would seem, is energy. Why not thoughts, feelings, and why not love?

Science recognizes that energy is never destroyed; it just changes its form. The energy from burning wood is converted into steam energy, the steam energy into locomotion, etc. Light, too, is energy. Energy is all around us. Energy is the building block of material. Seemingly solid objects are made of atoms, for example, and atoms contain atomic moving particles such as electrons. The electrons move around a nucleus. A table may appear and feel solid and without motion, but in truth, it is moving. Burn that same table and it creates energy in the form of heat. Everything is moving.

Things of substance are energy; we are made of energy. We are love. I surmise that, just as steam drives a locomotive, there is much about us that is driven by love. We thrive when we love and are loved. We sustain ourselves in love. We are happier when we love and are loved. We are inspired, motivated, healed and energized by love. When we love we are more creative, more passionate. Much of our music and poetry are of love.

If this is true, then that energy that is love exists all around us. It is us. It is another form of energy and like other forms of energy, it cannot be destroyed. It exists on earth and throughout the universe. It is powerful. I believe that love is God and God is love. He is the energy from whence we came and to which we will return. When we *are drained and exhausted, when we are down and depressed, we need to be refueled with love.*

One need only look into the eyes of parents cuddling their children to know that there is energy there. Love is not just a feeling; it is energy. Love transforms into tender loving care for the child and the labor to nourish the child. Love turns into deeds and deeds nurture the child. It is one of the many things that scientists can neither see nor perceive, except through the behavior of those who love. There are no meters or gauges to measure it. CAT scans cannot detect it. Yet, its existence is undeniable. Scientists may deny that love is energy, yet they cannot deny that love accomplishes many things. Love can and has influenced the course of human events.

If we are love, when we die we return to that state that we were at before our birth, as the iron ore returns to the earth. We become energy again. We become love. We are not destroyed; we continue to exist, but in a different form. We return to the ambient energy, love, all around us. We return to God.

I thought about this as I looked out over the windward side from the Pali and marveled at the panoramic magnificence before me, the endless and relentless blue Pacific Ocean, the verdant jungles and manicured golf courses, the mystical clouds and the soaring Koolaus. I thought when I die, I will return to this. How beautiful!!!

I want you to print this out and think about it. Many will not agree with this, but this is what I believe. Many will call this hokey or Pollyanna, but I find it reassuring and I believe it is true. In my lifetime I have been richly rewarded when I chose genuine love. My wife and my children have been my greatest prize, my greatest reward and my finest success. They are the proof of everything I just said. If I had attained wealth and fame and not achieved this, I would have achieved nothing.

When I put you to bed and whispered that I loved

you, you would ask me why I always repeated that. Now you know. I was renewing and reenergizing myself.

I love you,

Dad

This would explain why we seek love. We want to be loved and we want someone to love. If we are energy and love is energy, then we are reenergized by energy, by love. Turning to love is like plugging in, like recharging our batteries. It is why a kiss, a hug and a touch can reinvigorate us. It is why a pretty little girl in a yellow dress can keep me dancing through the night. It is as real as radio waves and photons, although invisible, they are real. All exist and all are energy.

Energy comes in many different forms, many that science has yet to identify. Steam energy turns into kinetic energy. Hydraulic energy converts to electrical energy. Pain is a feeling; pain is electrochemical energy conducted along neuro pathways. Love is a feeling, too. Even solid objects -- the earth, the table, the girders in a stadium -- are all energy.

Although thought, it is seldom said: Love is an end in and of itself. We long for it from the time we are born and thrive on it until we die. It is up there with eating and breathing. Love thrills us, sustains us and renews us. We seek to give it and we seek to receive it. Just as electricity flows in circuits, so must love. We celebrate love in our songs, ballads, poems and writings. Love is the vital and indispensable ingredient of happiness. We are happiest when we are in love.

Children have more energy than adults. Their energy is fresh and new and seemingly infinite. Perhaps this is why a little cherubic face staring up at us from the crib keeps us coming back. They are batteries that we plug into.

CHAPTER EIGHT

Teddy Bear Blues, Eraser Caper

"In this and in so many such wonderful ways, little girls would break down their fathers and train them into being warm and cuddly and soft, even after a hard day at the office."

Just a month before Christmas 1990, my oldest daughter, Kelly, dragged down the stairs two large lumpy garbage bags. The movement and the sound of the plastic bags tumbling down the stairs and dragging on the floor caught my attention.

"What's in there?" I asked.

Not seeming to hear me she continued to drag her lumpy secret into the family room. Curious, I moved off of the sofa and followed her into the family room. Again I inquired, "What's in there?"

She looked up at me with some trepidation, and with great feeling in her voice responded, "Daddy, I would like to make other children happy; those who are less fortunate and who do not have a father who can afford to give them presents."

With that response, she reached into her bag and drew out large and small teddy bears, old and treasured friends of Christmases past. "I want to make other children happy by donating these teddy bears," she said while dropping her voice as though not really wanting to be heard.

At this point a good parent would have choked back tears of joy at this display of charity from their 16-year-old daughter. Most would have been moved by such kindness from a teenager. It was an opportunity that cried out for some parental reinforcement, words of encouragement, tender and supportive words and words of reassurance for such a kind and giving nature. It was, without doubt, a cherished opportunity for good old dad to take her in his arms and express such sentiments.

Oh, how pitifully did this dad fail! Instead of offering these expressions, I exclaimed loudly in dismay, "How can you give away these old friends?! I gave many of them to you in past Christmases." I stood over her in disbelief, not knowing what else to say. After a brief silence shattered by the loud looks of others standing by, I realized what I had done. Feeling sorry for myself, I slunk quietly up the stairs. I prepared myself to be received by my bed and quietly, without even the customary good nights, slipped under the covers to wallow in my self pity.

Over many past occasions, I had personally chosen with the greatest care and thought some of these teddy bears. As I did so, I visualized how happy my daughter would be when she unwrapped each of them. I had personally made sure that my fuzzy purchases were without disease and dental caries. They were inspected from paw to paw. Each had been personally interviewed and found to come from good families. They had to be suitable for my little girl. I had enjoyed every look and expression when my daughter unwrapped these teddy bears over many Christmases. How could she part with these gifts that had been so carefully chosen for her?

So, I lay quietly in bed, even before the normal hour for sleep, with moist eyes searching the darkness of the ceiling and my heart for an explanation for this shameful behavior.

"Dad, do you want to see the new erasers I got." Erin asked pleadingly.

When Erin was just about eight years she would collect these specially designed erasers. Yes, I said erasers. These erasers did not come at the end of a pencil. They were not intended for erasing graphite markings on paper. These erasers were intended to be collected by children for boasting rights and privileges. Retailers would offer erasers of every size, shape, color and smell imaginable. They came in the shape of cars, trains, flowers, ice cream cones, bears, dolls, toys, alphabets and so on. Children would buy, collect, display, exchange and trade them. Most of all they were displayed, or rather shown off, to be admired by others. Erin was one of these avid collectors. So every time she got some new erasers she would be busting to show them off, and if you happen to be in the way at the time, you were bound to receive a tugging invitation to inspect and openly admire them.

It was not enough to just show off these erasers. They had to be displayed in plastic cases suited specifically for that purpose. So it was no surprise that whenever a birthday or Christmas approached, Erin would broadcast to the world precisely what she wanted for a gift. She wanted erasers or she wanted those plastic display cases called caboodles. Each tray in a caboodle had little compartments into which these little erasers fit perfectly. When a proud collector opened her case, the different trays at different levels would rise up, and their little compartments would reveal all of the treasured erasers that had been lovingly stored by little hands.

Any visitor or guest to our home could become a victim of an invitation, enthusiastically given, to inspect Erin's collection. The guest then was obliged to go up to Erin's room for an official viewing. It was not enough to view them passively. A quick glance would not suffice. Her pleading eyes and round face pressed the question and made it very apparent that one must gasp and be very amazed at each item displayed by her, one eraser at a time. Every time little Erin would point to one eraser or hold another up for a closer look, she would search each face to extract some sign of amazement or pleasure. Always, she would ask, "Do you like it?" She would ask her question while holding your face captive in her gaze. The question was always asked in such a way that the person simply had to like it or risk disappointing her. She would repeat her question after each item was examined, smelled, palpated, prodded and admired. One would have to be cold indeed not to feel the expectation there, and not to know the proper response.

Erin's enjoyment of anything was always marked by her need to share her joy. Unless it was shared, even with the most unwilling victim, her joy would be incomplete. She needed to see a smile and a gush of pleasure. Erin enjoys things better when others enjoy them, too. This put a lot of pressure on friends and even strangers who understood this. Good friends, indeed, all considerate people with any semblance of a heart, were put in the position of either enjoying it or disappointing Erin, such was the danger upon entering our house. Erin was always a trap waiting to be sprung upon anyone with the courage to call at our house.

She carried this into her adulthood. If she liked a movie, she would go to see it again, with close friends in tow. But this time her eyes would not be on the screen. They would be fixed on the illuminated faces of those who had accompanied her. She enjoyed things a second time, and time and time again, vicariously through the overt enjoyment of others. Old jokes became new again upon her hearing the fresh laughter of friends and family.

When she reported to me that a touching scene in the film "Whale Rider" brought tears to the eyes of her then-boyfriend, Tyrone, I was reassured that he was a good and compassionate person. Her ability to mine the feelings of others through their expressions is a strength that assists her in making sound judgments about people. When she reports to me the reactions of others, I know I can trust her judgment.

So it was then that her dad, living in the same house, was always available to admire her erasers -- a convenient person to accept her many invitations. He was her last resort when no other victims were nearby. Holding up an eraser she had shown me so many times before, she would say, "Look at this one, Dad. Don't you think this one is pretty?" Certainly, precious moments like these are not uncommon when the adult mind searches to find some adult reason to appreciate something that only a child can find so much delight in. The significance of such moments easily escapes the distracted, busy parent. An adult answer here would not serve that special moment between a dad and his little daughter. There is tension between an honest answer and the more diplomatic answer. Dads quickly learn that a truthful answer is not always the best response, and sometimes there is goodness in holding back what's really on his mind. The moment calls for an effusive, affirmative answer. It is also urgent that the answer be short so as not to prolong the session. "Yes, it is." I would hear myself blurting out with feigned enthusiasm. This answer would be routinely issued over and over again like a mantra. The canned answer was the best way to survive these repeated questions put to a weary brain conflicted with other matters of seemingly greater importance. The response, however, had to be expressed in convincing fashion for though Erin was just a child she was precocious; she had an ability to perceive when the response was genuine or not. Good acting had to be practiced when responding to her questions, and, indeed, after countless questions of the same kind, I had become expert at it.

In this and in so many such wonderful ways, little girls would break down their fathers and train them into being warm and cuddly and soft, even after a hard day at the office. It is times like these when dads are forced to confront the conflict between what seems so important and what is really important. It is times like these that children with their little hands, and their little entreaties and their trouble-free minds help us cast away the stress of adult worries. All of these little moments, collectively, are what make raising children so enjoyable. Joy and happiness can be found in a plastic caboodle and in colorful little erasers, in little lies and children's eyes. They are in the minds and hearts of little children. The greatest blessing children bring is the daily reminder of what is truly important. Somehow, we lose the knack when we grow up.

Children are the gyroscopes of their parents. They are daily reminders that all problems pale in contrast to the loss of any one of them. I do not want to survive my wife and children. am not as afraid of death as I am of not seeing them again. Never seeing them again is my greatest fear. Children provide the balance and perspective on life that keep us from straying off course and making derelicts of our lives.

In the blink of an eye, little Erin grew into a high school student. She wanted to go on a trip to the Midwest, the East

Coast and to Europe with her theater group at the Castle High School Performing Arts Center. To get our permission she had to agree to earn and save most of the money she would need to make this trip. She participated in all types of fund-raising events, including car washes and running for pledges. One of the events required rummaging through our attic for unwanted treasures to sell at large sales on campus. Erin started collecting these items in our living room.

"What is this?" I asked as I passed through the living room.

"Dad, those are my erasers."

"Why are they out here?"

"I'm going to sell them at the garage sale." She replied.

"How can you sell them? You spent so much of your time saving and collecting them. I don't think you should sell them," I heard myself saying.

"But... Dad, I am sure there are many people with children who would like them, and I need to make more money for my trip," she replied, sensing that this was important to me.

"Wait a moment. How can you sell them? You can save them and give them to your own children. I am sure they are valuable now and will be more valuable then."

I could not believe I heard myself saying this to my high school daughter who was willing to part with her own cherished property in order to pay for her trip. Here she was using her own creativity and resources to make some money to attain her goal. This was much more important. Yet, here I was trying to talk her out of it. The urge to press the argument seemed uncontrollable.

Any lessons that I had learned from the teddy bear caper were nowhere to be found.

"Dad, I'll think about it. OK?"

With that I went back up to my room to retire for the night convinced that she was not going to sell those erasers. How could she?

The next morning when I came down from my room, I noticed that Erin was gone and the house was quiet. The items intended for sale were also gone, so were her erasers. Erin had decided to sell those erasers. She was actually going to sell those erasers! Those erasers were too important, I thought. Those erasers mean too much to her, I groused. I walked to and fro, incredulous and dejected. Then I got an idea.

I called an old client of mine who lived within a mile of Erin's school. David was surprised to hear from me, for we had not seen nor talked to each other for years. After a little catching up, I asked,

"David, could you please do me a favor? This will sound a little crazy, but it is very important to me."

I acquainted him with the history of the erasers and how those crazy erasers had come to mean so much to Erin. As I discussed this with him, it became increasingly clear that the erasers had somehow become more meaningful to me than to Erin. Who was I fooling, anyway? I mean after all, Erin was willing to part with them. It was I who did not want to see her part with them.

I asked, "Could you and Alice go down to Castle and buy those erasers from her? I'll reimburse you. You should not identify yourselves. You should be very casual about this and not incur her suspicion. You should not let on that you are purchasing those erasers at my request. You may want to come up with a credible story about why you want to purchase them. You can then bring them to me for safe keeping and I will give them back to her for Christmas. You should act quickly before someone else buys them!"

David thought it was a grand idea, and yes, they would like to be part of the scheme. He said that they would be on their way right after we hung up.

I whiled away the morning reading the newspaper, fidgeting and worrying that some other person may have beaten David to the erasers, and they and their precious caboodles would be lost to us forever. It was some time after lunch that I received a jubilant call from Erin. Her voice, which was usually at a higher volume than most, was soaring with excitement. She spoke as though she had closed the deal of her life and she was in disbelief.

"Dad, I'm calling from Tisha's cellular phone. You won't believe what just happened!"

"What?" I asked, feigning ignorance and trying to stem my rising excitement.

"Tisha, Yvette and I had displayed all of our items for sale. Then after awhile an elderly Japanese couple came by. They were really nice. They looked at my erasers. Guess what? They bought all of them." The amazement in her voice was obvious.

"All of them? You're kidding." I exclaimed, playing my surprise to the hilt.

"No, I'm not. They really bought all of the erasers. They said that their grandchildren would love to have them and so they wanted them all. Everyone was totally surprised. Tisha was just....well, she started talking up the price."

"I can't believe it. What did they give you?" I asked.

"They paid more than $200 for everything."

"$200!" I exclaimed in genuine surprise for that was more than I had suggested to David.

"Yes...more than $200, and everyone is talking about it."

Indeed, news of the transaction had spread throughout the campus and had reached legendary proportions. Months later I would hear friends and teachers talk about it. No one believed that those erasers would sell so quickly and would fetch such a high price.

A few days later, when I returned to my office, a large box containing the erasers was sitting on my desk. David had dropped the box off earlier. I kept it in my office for the next six months waiting for the moment when Erin would unwrap the box by the Christmas tree. Everything had to be just right for the opening. The scene had to be set and the characters in place. As Shakespeare has written, "The plan is afoot and now the thing." Could I keep the secret and restrain myself until the time was right?

Christmas in our home is always big, but this season would be special. There would be a special surprise that Erin could not easily erase (pun intended) from her memory. Even though our youngest was now in high school, we strived to keep Christmas a special time for all. As my children grew older this became a big challenge. The unveiling of the ruse had to occur under special conditions. We did not want the unwrapping of the erasers to override the usual family customs that were observed on Christmas day. We decided that the affair had to be sprung on a day before Christmas and with the people who were closest to Erin at the time the plot went down. That would be Tisha and Yvette. Erin's emotions are always heightened and made more dramatic when she is surrounded by good friends.

Tisha and Yvette were her best friends and were unabashedly emotional about almost anything that was a surprise. Tisha is, in fact, the queen of surprises; her surprise parties, her pranks, and personally creative gifts are legendary. Tisha was her oldest and wisest friend whose emotions and flamboyant behavior were almost always genuine and unbridled. She was so genuine, open and expressive that any secret confided to Tisha could not but be read in her face despite her best efforts to conceal them.

I recall a time when I actually sang to Tisha when it was just the two of us in the living room. Sang is not the correct word; "inflicted" is probably the better description of what I did to Tisha. To her surprise I burst into a song, and deliberately revealed my inability to carry a tune. In truth, she brought it upon herself by asking me to sing to her, not thinking that I would actually do so. Now, it is not in my nature to expose people to such brutal punishment, but I thought that, in the case of Tisha, it would be great fun, and it was. As the mangled notes tripped from my lips like Irishmen leaving a pub, I fixed my gaze on Tisha's face so tightly that it was near impossible for her to look away from me. I was an expert at using this device, for I have done it so often in attempts to read jurors. I held her eyes captive in my unblinking gaze as I attempted to sing with all the seriousness of a true virtuoso feigning all the while that I was really into my performance, that I really was convinced that I excelled at it. It took all the little acting skills that I had to keep a straight face. To have at any time broken the song with laughter would have let Tisha off too easily. I was rewarded then and to this day with the image of the strain that played on her face second by second, as she struggled mightily to hold her smile and disguise her suffering. Tisha had to muster all the charity and mercy of a good Christian to continue the pretense that she was enjoying my performance. It was one that no layman with even the slightest musical appreciation could listen to without feeling that discomfort familiar to those who have eaten something excruciatingly disagreeable. While I continued to pinion her eyes in my gaze, Tisha bravely held up the corners o her smile, which seemed to fidget as though wanting to give way to the gravity of the truth. Her eyes tried to roll away from my gaze, but could not. There was palpable panic behind her expression as she seemed to struggle to spare me from the hur she must have thought the awful truth would bring me. Here was just one instance of a Christian being tested beyond the limits: to reveal the truth behind her pain and thereby stop the pain, or to reflect compassion and charity by disguising it and thereby extending her suffering. If I read her mind, I am sure that more than one prayer for mercy passed through it, even a thought that this persecution was a heaven-sent trial that could determine in what place her soul would go for all eternity. I did everything I could not to smile or laugh at the conflicting emotions washing over her visage. She had summoned the aid of every muscle in her face to save me from the truth. She held her smile through those tortuous moments, but the relief on her face when it ended was almost too much for me to bear, to kee from falling down and laughing. I could almost hear the relief as she took a breath and every muscle in her face relaxed as though thankful that the source of so much of her discomfort had ended. It may have been cruel to have tried Tisha so, but i was such a delicious memory for me that I would do it again.

Tisha is an attractive church leader, a youth and women's leader and all-round charismatic personality chock full of talent. Without fail, her personality could jump out of her body and run amok in any room she entered, totally naked for all to see. Nor was the enforced quiet of a library or movie house spared her roaring laughter. Some happy prankster had pilfered the volume-control knob on her. When she laughed, anyone within a mile would know it.

Yvette, like Tisha, has a heart as big as a barn. She has the voice of an angel when she lets out with a song.

When the three of them would laugh together, all the neighbors would know there was a ruckus at our house. That is exactly what was required for this Christmas surprise: the high octane, high volume, adrenaline-charged excitement that they, together with Erin, generate. They were the perfect ingredients for springing my scheme. Besides, they had been present when the now legendary heist took place and the "elderly Japanese couple" was supposedly taken advantage of. What moral scruples tried their Christian consciences, I wondered, as they believed they were fleecing this unknowing, Japanese couple? Yes, they absolutely had to be part of the unwrapping ceremony.

David and Alice, my co-conspirators, also had to be there at the unwrapping, but how? Would they be recognized and the plot uncovered before the unwrapping of the erasers? There was no option. They were integral to the plot, and besides, when the entire affair was first hatched, I had promised them that they would be included. The surprise could not be complete without all the conspirators present. David and Alice were essential; they had to be there.

The time had been set and my other children let in on the secret so that they would be prepared to witness the surprise and enjoy the event with full understanding. We concocted an excuse to have a party to include Tisha and Yvette about a week before Christmas. It would be a brunch, and arrangements were made to have all assembled before our traditionally tall Christmas tree.

David and Alice were invited. We concluded that David and Alice would not be recognized by any of the girls because it had been more than six months since the purchase had taken place, and the entire transaction was brief. David was enthusiastic when accepting the invitation. We agreed on some credible explanation about their presence at the party. They were to arrive at the door with gifts and explain that they just happened to be in the neighborhood delivering gifts. I would invite them in to join us for the meal. If confronted with questions, they were prepared to put off any suggestion that they had ever seen or met the girls before.

Since the brunch was supposedly for Erin and her two best friends, mom threw herself into preparing the food in earnest. The table was decorated and mom put out sumptuous eatables. Everything was done to give no hint of the main event. The house was filled with the smells of sizzling bacon, eggs, a Christmas tree, music and coffee when Tisha and Yvette arrived. The girls hugged and chatted and filled themselves with the offerings on the table. Soon, there was a knocking at the door. It was David and Alice dressed in their finest aloha attire. I expressed great surprise at seeing them. Greetings were exchanged, and David explained his "passing through the neighborhood" story.

Everyone was now standing near the door. As I introduced David and Alice to everyone, I noticed Tisha with her face slightly screwed up as though there had been a flicker of recognition. This is not unusual with Tisha for whenever a feeling emerges from any part of her it seems to shout out from every pore in her body. If she had any weakness, it was that she was nearly incapable of hiding her feelings. She started raising her index finger and screwing up her face as though she recalled something and wanted to pose a question. Erin and Yvette also began to wrinkle their brows as though struggling with an emerging sense of recognition. When Erin asked if they had ever met before, I moved quickly to change the subject.

"Of course, Erin may remember David and Alice from when she was a lot smaller," I said. "I was David's attorney at one time and both had been over to our house a long time ago." David quickly nodded agreement.

As I said this, I ushered everyone into the room hoping that the action would divert them from thinking much more about the flickering recognition. I was successful. I was able to distract the girls from the question and deflect any follow-up questions. My answer seemed to satisfy Erin, and the conversation between David and I quickly turned to news of our families since we had last met.

During this time, everyone assembled in the living room, and any signs of suspicion or recognition disappeared. Tisha, Yvette and Erin were sitting on the floor together, and David and Alice sat on the sofa. Mom, Kevin and Kelly were sitting around the breakfast table in front of the girls, a perfect vantage point to capture all the expressions when the surprise was sprung. The stage had been set and the time had arrived. All was perfect for springing the trap. I took over the conversation.

"We wanted to have this little special party to honor Erin's very good friends, Tisha and Yvette, and so we would like to present each of them with some gifts, just tokens of our gratitude for their friendship. Merry Christmas to each of you."

As I made this announcement, I handed each of them gifts previously prepared and wrapped by mom.

"My gosh, thank you," said Tisha and Yvette.

After what seemed to me like hours, they began to unwrap their gifts without any idea that the main event was yet to come. Thinking back on it, the moment was too brief. I should have been patient, but I was too anxious to move quickly to the event I had been waiting for for more than six months. I should have let that moment play out a little longer to savor it more. I should have allowed a little more time for the plot to develop. Instead, I rushed it by saying, "You know, Erin, maybe, you should open a gift under the tree. We don't want you left out. We will give you permission to unwrap a gift before Christmas." At this, I stood up, reached over and pulled out from under the tree the box of erasers that had been wrapped in Christmas paper.

All eyes were now fixed on Erin. Yvette and Tisha were still unsuspecting. Erin had no clue. But those who were in on it hung on every passing second. Kelly had her camera at the ready. My co-conspirators were at the edge of the sofa. Erin began to unwrap the gift. It had been wrapped and under the tree for weeks leading up to this moment. Now, suddenly, it was thrust before her and it wasn't even Christmas day. Erin was clearly surprised to be given a gift to unwrap so early, and she was beginning to wonder why so much attention was being paid to her actions. She removed the wrapping but did not seem to recognize the box. It was the original box she'd put all her erasers into before selling them to that elderly couple. I held my breath as she struggled with the tape. She finally opened the box at one end and peeled back the flaps. All eyes were still on her. It was quiet, except for the sound of the pulling of ribbons and tearing of paper.

She peered into the box and saw what she had thought she would never again lay eyes on. She had thought they were gone forever, out of her life, never again to be hers.

"Oh my gosh," she cried as her hands covered her mouth, and tears began to flow.

Everyone who was in on it suddenly broke out laughing and applauding.

"What is it?" asked Tisha, seeking to understand the reason for so much laughter. She and Yvette looked into the box in turn, and as recognition slowly dawned, their faces turned red and more tears came to join the tears of Erin. Click! went Kelly's camera. The moment was captured. The erasers were back, right in their laps. Right in the box on the floor before them were the erasers that they had gotten more than fair price for by taking advantage of two doting grandparents, the Japanese couple. Japanese couple? And there they were. The girls began pointing at David and Alice, who were smiling and sitting right next to them, as the sorting and sifting of clues developed into a recognition of who these impromptu guests were and why they had seemed so familiar.

"You..." Tisha gasped, still pointing with an outstretched arm and her finger moving up and down with the excitement from the recognition.

"You were the ones," said Yvette, now also pointing at the couple as the meaning of all of this became clear to her also.

Erin sat there on the floor. Tears were still pouring from her eyes as she tried to take in and understand what was happening, how it was that the erasers had been returned to her in this manner. The realization was quick in coming. It came as fast as her tears. She had been played.

The story of the elderly couple that had paid too generously for the erasers had spread through the campus and was now legend, except now the legend had to be amended. The story had to be corrected. History had to be rewritten. It was a prank, and as it turns out, Erin was the lucky victim, not the "nice Japanese couple."

And dad had his way. He turned the memories of that lovable little collection into family lore, never to be forgotten, and he still contributed to sending his littlest daughter to Europe. He turned a moment of a father's sadness into a surprise, a time as priceless as every moment with his children is priceless to a father. It was a moment to remember. It was warm and fuzzy. It was a special Christmas. It was our family.

How I wish I could stare into those big eyes again as she asks me, "Dad, do you like it? Huh? Do you like it?" I want those moments back.

Is it ungrateful of me, having been given these moments, to want even more? Is it selfish to always want more?

If anyone could resemble Tinker Bell of Never Never Land, it is our Erin. It seems she skipped before she ever learned to walk. She would rather skip and laugh than walk about. She skipped to the door when answering a knock. She skipped up the stairs to her room; she skipped at every opportunity. She has an active mind. Her tongue loses every time it tries to keep up with her racing thoughts. She will quite vanquish the most amicable ears with her cascade of bedeviling and unsettlingly endless, rapid sequence of questions, one following quickly the other.

"Dad, I found this black leather jacket hanging in your closet. I've never seen you wear it. May I have it?"

Disquieting silence followed as I searched for an answer, one that would be tactful. That leather jacket had been given to me by my father.

"You don't use it. Why can't I have it? It's just hanging there. I like it. May I have it?"

I paused. She was right. I don't use the jacket, and yes, it was just hanging there. She had deftly started laying the groundwork to weaken my resistance.

"No." I said. I was afraid to disappoint her and wanted to let her down softly, but she was not going to reciprocate by softly letting up. Erin's greatest attribute is her determination and persistence. Couple that with her rapid-fire questions and loud voice and you have the ingredients for great danger. Anyone in her line of fire might be readily forgiven for beseeching heaven to be spared: "Why me?".

"But, Dad....Why not? You don't use it at all, and it looks good on me." She was right, of course. It did look good on her. Most things look good on her. Most anything looks bad on me. It was a below-the-belt implication.

"Otherwise, it will just hang there and not be used." It would have been futile to point out to her that many things just hang in the closet and are not used for long periods. That does not mean that they needed to be gifted so that they would not die of boredom. My need to conserve time and energy as a busy professional is what made me so vulnerable to Erin's persistence. Persistence is needed to resist persistence. That morning I had very little persistence. Erin is as persistent as the Saharan winds, over time even rocks erode. I was hopelessly vulnerable.

"Why not?" Now she is pressing me with her big brown eyes, one of her most charming features, and one she used to good advantage when trying to charm something out of her father.

"No." I repeated. Now I've lost my place in the newspaper I had been reading.

"But, Dad......why not?" Her voice was now trailing and dropping plaintively off, her little way of seeming to be wounded Perhaps, a little cry of pain would help chip away at my resistance.

"Nope." said I, truncating my answer in an attempt to put a period to this conversation. I've lost my concentration at this point and am wondering what I was reading.

"But, Dad, it makes no sense that this leather jacket should be hanging in your closet unused." Now she has decided to take half a pie.

"May I hang it in my closet?" she asked, thinking to herself that that was a reasonable request, and once it's in her closet the passage of time and my poor memory will make it hers. Possession, of course, eventually becomes ownership. If I was not going to give her ownership now, she would at least take possession. Certainly, dad can't object to that.

"I like that jacket." I explained realizing now that this subject was not going to die quickly, and given my vulnerability that morning, I was in serious danger of going the way of the rocks in the Sahara desert.

"But....Dad...you never wear it." she said sensing that her simple logic was taking hold.

"Look, Kung Kung gave that jacket to me. I like it."

"Dad, the last time you wore it was when we went to Oregon years ago. Let me put it in my closet. That's all. Just let me put it in my closet."

"But why do you want it in your closet?"

Sensing victory, for I'm showing that I am anxious to get back to reading, she answers, "I just want people to see it in my closet."

"If that's so important to you .... OK," I blurted out, surrendering what to me seemed so trivial anyway. The jacket would be in her closet but in the same house; I can always retrieve it. "What difference does it make what closet it is in?" I rationalized. I just wanted to resume whatever it was I was doing, reading whatever it was I was reading and enjoying whatever it was I was enjoying.

"Thanks, Dad." She said as she jumped up and kissed me, suspecting that it was the beginning of that jacket becoming hers. The intent of the kiss was not so much from affection as it was to seal the deal.

Shifting her attention from this conquest with amazing alacrity she calls out to her brother who is just then leaving through the front door, "Kevin, did you try on that shirt that the Eisenbeis gave you?"

"No, stupid." Kevin shot back as he usually does, taking great pleasure in irritating his sisters. He is always at the ready to provoke a fight with them, particularly the youngest. Erin has learned to give it right back.

"Hey, fat pig, it probably doesn't fit you anyway. May I have it? Huh, may I have it?"

CHAPTER NINE

Wife, Mother, Lover

"There are two questions that have perplexed me for all these many years of our marriage: Why you married me and why, having discovered the terrible mistake, you stayed with me."

It is impossible not to mention at greater length the woman who was most responsible for bringing these strangers into the world and into my life. She is my indispensable partner. She gives true meaning to the words "your better half." She was the one most responsible for their daily nurture, care and upbringing. It was her patience, unselfish love and loving tutelage that made them who they are today. I owe my family and my happiness to her.

Carol never lets things bother her, and in that rare instance when she does, she never lets it stay around for long. She is always solicitous to the needs of her children and to her impatient husband. When I was single I had no idea how incomplete I was until I met her and she supplied the rest of what makes me whole.

Taped on the back of the kitchen cabinet door is a note to herself in her own handwriting as a ready reminder of her resolve to lose weight. It was placed where she would see it if she should ever attempt to sneak a snack.

Jan. 8   11:58 p.m.

I, Carol Chang, firmly resolve to lose 10 pounds by March 1. I will do this by dulling my interest in food, except where necessary for my health.

More -- milk and water

Less -- meats and snacks

NO -- desserts and dips

I will attempt to take short, brisk walks after dinner regularly.

I will not think about the pleasures of eating. If I have a special meal planned I will spend the time prior to it in a state of near fast (i.e. water, vegetable sticks, Swiss cheese and distracting activities).

Instead of eating a sneaky snack, I will write letters, for example...

THIS TIME I MEAN IT!!!!!!!

Next to this personal note, she taped a silhouette of a rather well-endowed, curvaceous figure provocatively posing with her head thrown back and voluptuous long hair draping down over her arms. This was to show Carol what she could look like, an incentive to ward off those evil little voices that tried to sate her unhealthy cravings with snacks. In my mind there was nothing wanting about my wife's figure, but I loved her for those tender intentions that devised such a humorous note.

Carol is always interested in people. People are always first in her mind and in her heart. That is why she enjoys writing her Waha Nui column in *MidWeek*. She finds the lives of people interesting and newsworthy. On the other hand, people are not as interesting to me. I often forgot their names seconds after they are introduced to me. Whenever I tell Carol that I met so and so, she asks me about their children, their relations, their occupation, and the schools they attended. I seldom have the answer to any of these questions. I don't even think to ask.

She is unselfish; she always put others first. When she serves a meal that may not quite be enough for all those at the table, she finishes her portion but waits to see whether everyone else is full before she takes more. After many years of marriage I began to sense when she does this. I eat a calculated portion and then I make a point of deliberately and noticeably rising from the table and taking my plate and utensils with me to the kitchen sink. This is a clear, unambiguous signal to Carol that I've had my fill and it's all right for her to eat the rest. I do this whether I'm full or not.

Watching Carol eat heartily is so satisfying. I think that this is a natural thing. Mothers and grandmothers get great satisfaction out of watching people they love, even good guests, fill themselves up and enjoy their cooking. Watching my children eat does this for me. It may be evidence that I'm carrying out my responsibilities as a father to provide for them. Their enjoyment of the food put before them is their way of thanking me. So whenever Carol goes on a diet, I'm disappointed because it deprives me of these moments of satisfaction.

Popcorn with additional salt and butter boosts Carol's enjoyment of movies at a theater. In the darkness, when her face is lit by the glow of the big screen, I sneak a peek at her raising a popped kernel to her mouth. I derive satisfaction from that just as I do when I hear her fussing with the dishes downstairs in the early morning, or speaking affectionately to our lovable, stinky mutt before leaving for work. So I'm a little disappointed whenever she decides to forego the popcorn. At times, when she refused to have it, I buy popcorn for myself and have the server put a double dose of butter on it. She has to sit and watch me enjoy eating it, as the crunch and the aroma drive her mad. I usually can't finish what I order, so I make a point of sliding the unfinished box under my seat. It's impossible to do it without her noticing. Soon, just as I expected, I sense her leaning over in the darkness of the theater, reaching down and groping for the box. I protest in a whisper, reminding her of her diet. She retorts that it should not be wasted. After all, there are a lot of people starving in the world and it is her calling to appreciate the abundance we have by consuming every morsel, to save it from seeing the bottom of the trash can.

At Chinese dinners it is customary to have a very little dish at each table setting for mustard and other sauces mixed with soy sauce. Diners with chopsticks dip food into this small dish to add flavor. Carol readily adopted this custom after I introduced her to it. She loves to dip her food into sauces. It is just part of the culture of eating a Chinese meal, just like using chopsticks. But to me, it's become a symbol of my wife's acculturation. When I was courting her, I introduced her to fine Chinese food; that and my seemingly sophisticated taste in good cuisine are, in part, what attracted her to me, she says. So I derive special enjoyment from watching her mix her mustard with soy sauce. It's one of the first things she does when sitting down for a Chinese meal. It is just another one of her little acceptances of the culture she had married into, and it is a nod to her love for me.

Carol was quick to adjust and to cope with the many changes that came her way when she married me. Her mother and father and uncles and aunties were tall Caucasians. That is what she was used to in her life in Oregon. When she first came to Hawaii, my family came over to the house to meet her, my future bride. They lined up to greet her. Carol said that one of the things that stood out for her was that she seemed taller than most of them, and when greeting them, she would have to look down. She stayed with my family for almost three months before our wedding, during which time, she quickly acclimated to the diversity of Hawaii.

When her relatives and friends began arriving days before the ceremony, she picked them up at the airport. She said that her first impression upon seeing them there was that they were so tall and pale.

It was a phenomenon that I could appreciate, for when I was attending law school in Oregon I experienced similar feelings. Through my three years in law school, I was the only Asian student in a sea of Caucasians. Maybe that's the primary reason I was accepted there, a token attempt at diversity. It certainly wasn't because of my academic credentials. But whatever the reasons, I was grateful. I did not encounter the slightest prejudice or discrimination; I was totally at home in this environment and I developed some very close friendships. We were all thrown together with one and only one common mission: to survive the rigors of our first year and to live to see another. Sharing that solitary mission, we studied, discussed, argued over and worried about nothing but the case decisions and subjects in our legal texts and from our lectures, and we did it all together. The law library became our home where, at times, we would stay into the very late hours, and the oral questions from professors at lectures became our common adversity. Although there were other Asian students on campus outside of the law school at the University of Oregon, my world was this little clique of white students in Fenton Hall, the building that housed our law school. They became my constant companions and the only people who understood the trials and difficulties of that environment. So it was that most of those months and years were spent with a steady diet of white comrades and white professors. It was easy for an Asian to lose his identity there.

So that is how it was when school was let out one Christmas season, and I agreed to spend that holiday with friends in San Francisco. When I visited Chinatown, I found myself strangely out of sorts and feeling insecure there. The Asian people walking on the streets, talking on the corners and shopping in stores seemed strange, and yes, even a little intimidating. Somehow, I had lost myself in that law school environment, and maybe, just maybe, momentarily forgot that I was Asian and that I did not look at all like my fellow law students. This curious feeling, passed very quickly, however, almost as fast as it had come over me. I believe it is some evidence that the outward shell that differentiates the races is, in fact, but an outward shell that dissolves very quickly with familiarity and friendship.

Carol had adjusted so well that her feet became flat and she grew unaccustomed to wearing shoes. She was able to understand the accents of locals in Hawaii better than I, and she spoke with them using the same inflections better than I. She worked very briefly for a small, local savings and loan firm privately owned by a Japanese family, and in that short time her employer and co-workers, who were mostly Japanese, developed affection for her and a respect for her work ethic.

I always like my toast heaped high with butter, peanut butter and strawberry preserves as a nighttime snack. Seeing me prepare this snack, Carol would complain and remind me of the high calorie count. Or sometimes she would say nothing, but turn up her nose at me as I prepared my dripping, oozing, fatty toast. It is such a ritual that whenever I'm in the kitchen making toast, I find myself pausing to look up at her. I pause to allow her a second to remark about excessive calories. I pause just to delight in hearing her disapproval. Sometimes I leave a piece on the plate, groaning with the heavy butter, peanut butter and preserves lathered all over it, and when I return minutes later, it has a bite mark on it. I complain and she denies everything with a guilty grin. Unless this house is haunted, there are no other possible culprits. Despite her looking down her nose at my peanut butter rituals, she sometimes feigns disappointment when I did not give her a bite of my toast. I try to remember to give her the last bite. My memory was never good from the start, but it's particularly faulty when I'm enjoying my snack. She softly utters her disappointment when I forget. Consequently, I force myself to remember to give her the last bite. When I hand her the plate with the little morsel, she pretends surprise and exclaims with delight. Just to hear that was worth my lost enjoyment of that last bite.

Although we are different in many ways, we are similar in ways that are important. We are compatible. We are a partnership. We fill in each other's weaknesses with our own strengths. Our compatibility allows us to be a team in raising children and conducting our household. When I am impatient, she is patient. When I am concerned about the future, she strives to keep us grounded in the present. When I am stormy, she is like an eddy, quiet and calm. When I lose perspective, she serves to quietly remind that I have and refuses to get caught up in my frenzy. When I worry about our finances, she fusses over the children's birthdays, their friends, their clothing, their meals and their school activities. When I lost sleep over a client's case, she slept with her children's disagreements, their everyday concerns, their requirements, needs and wants. When I did not want to be concerned about the small stuff, she saw them to be the big stuff that they were. What I see as unimportant, she sees as important -- to her children and to others. I never like the minutiae, so she manages the bank statements and bills. Where I am quick to strike back and criticize or offend, Carol seldom utters a word of complaint. I have never heard her maliciously say something unkind about anyone, although I have no compunction about doing it myself. She never utters an invective or obscenity; she is always proper and restrained. I, on the other hand, see an obscenity as a permissible way of putting an exclamation point where emphasis is required, in the proper company, of course. While I seethe about an offense, Carol is quick to forgive. When I look for an ally, her good example infuriated me. I make the major decisions on our investments, insurance, retirement accounts, finances and real estate purchases; she let me.

Because Carol is such a good wife and mother, and because she enjoys every second of being a mother, she took good care of our children and our home. I never had to worry about how things were going at home. She never complained about anything even when I returned from work very late in the evening or from a long business trip. She never let the difficulties of raising three children be anything but a joy, and I never ever saw her feeling sorry for herself. She enabled me to realize success in my career and to make the gains I did to support our family, but unless there is any doubt, Carol was the person responsible for their care, nurture, raising and upbringing. My profession as a trial attorney was a jealous mistress that consumed all of my time, at work and at home. Because of Carol, I was enabled to be a father as well as an attorney. My children are who they are largely because of their mother.

As our children grew into adults, and the results of her maternal efforts became apparent, I realized that the small stuff that she handled was not small at all. Despite the difficulties my jealous profession presented, Carol did not allow herself to be bothered by them. She derived so much joy, pleasure and fun from raising her children that it never occurred to her to want to be anywhere else or to do anything else. It was apparent to all, including our children, that Carol was in heaven when her life was full of her family. Children are born with a keen sense for genuine love and they know that their mother's love comes from a very real place in her heart.

When most people would arrange and decorate their homes in a manner so as to impress guests, Carol would do it to make her home more, well, homey. I was one of those who wanted my home to impress others. So my thinking was that only our best photos and paintings should be hung on the walls. I thought walls were reserved for the exposition of good paintings, fine handcrafted batiks and other artful wall hangings. I was dismayed when Carol simply tacked up pictures of our family, paintings and scribbling made by our children, a certificate of award for the World's Greatest Mom given to her by Erin, the foot and hand prints of our children in different colors made over various years, certificate of the World's Greatest Father by Kelly and notes and cards to us from our children. She did this despite my protests. Over time I began to appreciate that what is important is not what others expected or thought of our home, but rather, how happily we live in our own home. Carol tacked up things that were meaningful to us, not to infrequent visitors. This is just another example of how she keeps me grounded in what is more important: our family.

This was brought home to me again when Erin, now fully grown and married, said that when she was younger, she was embarrassed when seeing the artwork of their childhood hung on walls to be seen by visitors. Later, however, she began to appreciate her mother's gesture when she learned that a childhood friend of hers had gifted a painting made by her own hands to her mother and later discovered it crumbled up and tossed in the wastebasket.

Carol makes me look good. Carol makes me look good when she holds my arm or stands next to me. She is beautiful. She is beautiful as my wife and beautiful as the mother of my children. She threw herself into motherhood, and she relished every moment. Not once, not for a second, did being a mother become an obligation, a chore or a responsibility. For her, being a mother was a daily celebration of life. She read every day to them, transported them to their school, to Cub Scout and Brownie meetings, camps and picnics, to soccer and swimming practices and competitions, to birthday parties and sleepovers. She bought them toys, books and clothes from garage sales and made building blocks from empty milk containers. She organized and played games with them and arranged events, activities and parties. By making my children who they are, she made me look good. I worked in the office, worked at my profession, and when I came home to my family, I took the bows and the applause although the credit belonged mostly to my wife. I enjoyed the results of her efforts. She enabled me to be a father despite the many stresses of my profession. Our children are what Carol has done, so she continues to make me look good. In fact, she has copy-edited this book, again to make me look good.

Motherhood may have delayed, but it did not deny Carol a career as a journalist. She is an excellent writer and a good journalist. A journalist is what she wanted to become. As Erin, the youngest of our children, grew to need less and less of her attention, Carol started working for a community newspaper part-time. That part-time job grew by increments to become full time as the children became more and more independent. Today, she is a respected, award-winning journalist, highly regarded by her readers. Her boss, the publisher of the paper, said about Carol: "A very large part of our success is Carol Chang. She is the mainstay of our community news, an aspect so important to MidWeek and something that really distinguishes us from all other local publications." Both houses of Hawaii's legislature have passed resolutions recognizing her exceptional service and qualities as a journalist.

Carol mostly wrote columns and feature articles for our community paper. She reports the excitement and meaning in a child's graduation, a student's receiving good grades, the recognition of a teacher's going above and beyond for the sake of her students, an act of kindness, a moment of extraordinary sacrifice and generosity, a community fund raiser, the bravery of a neighbor, the patriotism of a young soldier, the everyday achievement of families, the marriage of childhood lovers, the birth or adoption of a child and the otherwise unsung kindnesses of the many individuals in a community. I would come to describe what she does as casting a bright light on the rose amidst the many prickly thorns. She has by her pen stoked the pride of parents, rewarded the unselfish efforts of many, illuminated acts of goodness and set them up as examples, and recognized many in the community whose unselfish contributions would otherwise have gone unnoticed. She has a way of capturing the essence of what was so important to others about the subject she is reporting on. She has won a faithful readership and the gratitude of many in the community.

Her writings and her career successes as a journalist are simply a mirror of her love for people. Her interest is and always has been in people. She brought to her profession the kindness, gentleness and compassion for human beings that serves her family so well. Through her articles and columns she serves her readers a large dose of that same goodness.

Yet, when she would discuss these matters with me, I would too often deem them too insignificant to merit my full attention. I was of the mind that what I did in my profession was even more consequential for in my work the lives of clients and a lot of money are always at stake. I was mistaken and that was my weakness. This is, however, the strength that she brings to our relationship and to the raising of our family. She recognizes that there is great beauty in seemingly little things that bloom every day by the thousands, but each thing means the world to someone forgotten, someone without a voice. Through her writings she gives them much-deserved acclaim; she gives them a voice by shining a light on their acts.

On a quiet Sunday morning, I sat at the family room table reading the newspaper and sipping coffee. It was so quiet and so peaceful. I felt so relaxed. Every so often I would gaze out through the sliding glass door at our tall graceful guava trees swaying in the trade winds. The smaller vegetation moved in and out of the shadows as the light played between the taller trees. I lost myself and my thoughts in that guava tree forest and the only sounds I could hear were the cooing of the doves, the chirping of the birds and the rustling of the leaves. I thought to myself that it was a meditative moment sent to me by God. I leaned back on the chair to savor the moment.

Suddenly, that comfortable, satisfying moment was shattered when my wife asked, "Dad, can you test me on my Hawaiian? Just read the English and I'll repeat the Hawaiian translation." With that she handed me the lined yellow sheets of paper upon which were handwritten sentences in Hawaiian with their corresponding English translation.

Pouting about the interruption of my quiet Sunday morning, I replied, "Carol, that's not the best way to learn to speak a language." One fault, or arguably strength, that I have is that I usually resist doing things that do not make sense to me. For example, I rebel against the idea of tucking the sheet and bed spread under the pillows before placing the mock pillows on top. The mock pillows, I reason, is for the very purpose of avoiding that trivial task. Washing window screens with soap and water is another pet peeve of mine. Brushing off the dust and grime should suffice; after all, we are not going to eat off of those window screens. Besides, the water just promotes corrosion and wood rot.

My wife carefully stores little plastic Disney figures and other knick knacks on a little ridge on the top of a paper towel holder that hangs loosely on hooks held tentatively by adhesive tape, and every time I pull out a towel the little figurines fall off, clattering onto the counter and the floor. It would be as though I had shaken a cliff and all the little Lilliputians fell off the edge to their death. Their little bodies would be strewn all over the counter and floor. It drove me to distraction. It was not an effective place to display these little figures or anything else for that matter because the towel holder was under the ridge of a kitchen cabinet below shoulder level. Anything on it would be concealed from view. A display out of view is no display at all. If things displayed there fell a number of times, a sensible person would not recreate the circumstances for it happening all over again. There were better places to put those little figures than such a shaky and precarious platform. It did not make sense to put them back in the same place every time they fell off, but that is what she did. Pulling on the paper towels is like pulling on the ring to a fragmentation grenade. There is bound to be an explosion. It seems sheer lunacy to put the ring back into the grenade and set up the trip wire after each explosion.

If a cheap ballpoint pen runs out of ink, it should be disposed of and not be placed back into a container with other perfectly good writing implements. Every time I want to retrieve a good pen to make a hasty note, I have to pull out and test about three or more pens before finding the one that serves my purpose. Life, it seems to me, is too short for that kind of useless exercise. Carol has no compunction about putting a totally useless pen right back into the holder waiting for that time when I would again have to fish through them until I found a useful writing instrument. It is as though she thought that if an inkless pen were placed in the holder and allowed to rest there, it would somehow regenerate ink.

Carol always reads a book or the newspaper when we watch television. There are not many programs that hold her attention. Predictably, she misses something said or part of the plot. When she does, she asks me to fill in the blanks. If I stop to fill in her blanks, I risk missing something crucial myself. Each time she puts such a question to me becomes a stressful challenge. This happens so often that I pay no attention to her questions, but not without suffering some discomfort of conscience for it.

That morning of the Hawaiian homework, I would have been more receptive if the request made sense and I felt it was worthwhile and productive.

She insisted, "I need this. This is how I (emphasizing the first-person pronoun) learn to speak another language." By emphasizing the first-person pronoun she hoped to preempt any arguments that it would be a waste of time, after all learning was a personal thing and this is how she learned.

She sat down on the love seat with her legs and feet up, arms clasping knees, preparing herself for the first sentence that would test her grasp of its meaning. There she sat waiting and looking at me expectantly, almost daring me not to participate in the exercise. At this point, I had not agreed to anything, but by adopting this posture and smiling expectantly at me, it seemed that she thought she could charm me into participating.

There is quality about Carol that is childlike and charming. It is a quality that attracted me to her from the start. She seems capable of shutting out the complexities and difficulties of the world around her. This was a quality that enabled her to set aside the stresses of decision making and leave it to me. It was a quality that enabled her to put up with the irritability and the grave face I would put on when confronted with real problems. It was a quality that empowered her to be a loving wife and mother. In the heat of battle, it was an annoyance, but it kept me from losing all perspective. Despite my struggle with the adversities in my professional life, she was occasionally able to draw me into this protective cocoon she wove around herself. It was a voice that said I was losing sight of what was important and that things were not as bad as I made it seem. When instructing and comforting children, this quality of Carol's was a big plus, and so, I guess, I was a beneficiary. What confounded me at times, however, was that it is not helpful to hear this voice while in a burning building.

As life with my wife fully acquainted me with her distaste for conflict, I would try to keep her away when I negotiated the price of a new car or when I had a grievance with a repairman or retailer, or whenever the situation was adversarial. Conflict and confrontation were the staple of my profession as a litigator. I was trained and paid to wade into disputes. My clients' interest hung on who won and lost. I could not walk away from disputes nor minimize their importance. To my clients there was nothing more important. When you live with someone, however, preventing her presence in such situations is not always possible. Whenever the situation of conflict came up, it always made Carol and my children uncomfortable. They would easily dismiss these episodes by agreeing among themselves that dad is just falling into his "horse's ass" temperament again. They would go into their "whatever" mode. At times like this, dads get very little support and little understanding.

The request was simple enough. I could easily allow five minutes of my time by speaking the English sentences and receiving her Hawaiian translation. This was a small task in return for a lovely, loving wife who had given me three wonderful children, years of loving and a happy home. I could do it quickly and in no time I could return to the contemplative moment I had been enjoying. Being the practical and logical kind of guy I am, however, I thought it would have been an ineffectual exercise, and therefore, a squandering of good Sunday morning time. In fact, I was convinced that this was not the way to learn a language.

I said, "Quiet repetition *by yourself* would be more effective. Rote memory is not what you need to develop. You should be developing the language areas of your brain. You should develop your visual and auditory senses. While you read the sentences to yourself, visualize them and hear yourself say them out loud. While you do this reflect upon their meaning. You should do it by yourself"

"No, this is the way I (again emphasizing the pronoun) do it, and besides, it won't take long and this would be a bonding moment." She said this insistently, and she was not to be deterred. The bonding moment argument was one she often resorted to to engender guilt in me whenever I did not want to do something with her. After all, what good husband would dare to be against more bonding with his wife? I was no fool, however; I saw it for what it was, a wily and sneaky female ploy to circumvent logic, besides there was that peaceful morning interlude that I wanted to savor.

I reluctantly took up the pages, noting that there were not too many sentences anyway, and besides, it would take me much longer to try to explain to her why her method was ineffective. She was clearly exhibiting an attack of stubbornness and had walled herself off from all reasoning. I capitulated.

I began by reading the first sentence, "The three of them need work." There. I had read the first sentence and this tribulation would soon be over.

As she heard the first sentence, her eyes rolled back and her head dropped into her waiting hands. A soft groan of pain issued from her lips and she pulled her legs up to her chest as though the first sentence was a cudgel and I was beating her with it. Stuttering and tripping over herself, she managed to utter the first Hawaiian word. She now began staring at the ceiling as though the answer was there to be found. Then she looked pleadingly at me as if wanting some morsel of a hint thrown her way. It seemed like a long minute passed before the second word came forth grudgingly and agonizingly from her contorted lips. Now, again looking up at the ceiling and then at me and then at the yellow sheets of paper I held in my hands, she went into another spasm of pain, pulling at her hair and at her chin. She fidgeted about on the sofa and then furtively looked at me as if pleading to be relieved of her suffering. I avoided eye contact and continued to stare down at the yellow pages. I soon caught myself contemplating what a life in irons for spousal abuse would be like, and as I did so I could feel my quiet Sunday morning begin to melt away as this beloved person's face was taken over by fear that if the next answer was wrong a scorching bolt of lightning would strike her down. After excruciating moments, out tumbled the third word. No sooner did that word fall than she looked at me pleading for reassurance that she was correct. As I looked into her suffering eyes, any hope of saving the rest of this beautiful Sunday morning melted like butter on a plate on a warm humid day.

Wanting to pick up the pace, I elected not to quibble with a few vowels. I read the next sentence, "They have a grandfather."

"What?" she asked.

I repeated the sentence.

"Oh, that must be wrong." she said. "I think I wrote that sentence incorrectly. The pronoun should be possessive."

Although I did not quite understand what it was she just said, I seized upon this admitted error like a cat pouncing on a mouse. If anything, I was adept at recognizing opportunities that dropped into my lap; this was one of them. I thought that this surely must be divine intervention, and I was not about to "look a gift horse in the mouth." To do so would demonstrate ingratitude, and I had no way of knowing if God would ever send such a blessing my way again.

"Maybe, you should take these sheets back and make the corrections." I said, trying as much as possible to appear understanding and helpful while holding my breath. There was a rush of relief when she concurred and took those pages back. The strain of those tortuous moments, and the fear that many more such moments would follow, drained from me as fresh joy rushed in to replace them. My Sunday morning was saved.

Feeling a sense of triumph and relief, I was emboldened to repeat, "Rote memory is not what you want to develop. Speaking a language requires a different kind of memory. You must develop the speech part of your brain. I suggest that you repeat the sentences out loud to yourself while visualizing what it looks like and what it means." I said this almost under my breath, fearing that I might reignite whatever it was that had interrupted the enjoyment of the morning. As I think back on it, that was a risky gambit. Fortunately, I got away with it.

Perhaps, to the reader, this incident was not worth the reading. It was just a brief event in more than thirty years of marriage. It was merely one of millions of such episodes in this long wonderful marriage. It was more memorable to me because I was the victor in this one, and because, as I think back on it, it was so funny to see my wife squirm on that sofa. It reminded me of me as a little boy suffering to recite the multiplication tables under the watchful gaze of a stern and unforgiving instructor holding up a threatening switch. .

That's just one story I recall whenever I need to lift my spirits. I saved my Sunday of peaceful reflection and stored away yet another bonding moment. I love that woman.

Dear Carol,

There are two questions that have perplexed me for all these many years of our marriage: Why you married me and why, having discovered the terrible mistake, you stayed with me. Although, perhaps, I may never know the answer to those questions, I do know that I am the undeserving beneficiary of your poor judgment. I know that, had you not been so mistaken, my life would not have been so happy, so wonderfully blissful.

When we recently had occasion to view some old pictures of ourselves so long ago, I was reminded of how many wonderful years of your life you shared with me. I hope never to have to be reminded again. I want to always cling to happiness knowing that "in my life I was loved by you."

Could you, would you, please be my Valentine?

Your Lover

In response, Carol wrote the following:

Dear Hubby, I too enjoyed reliving our early days through those photos, because I know that around you good friends and good times sprout and grow.

You will always be my Valentine and I'm continually amazed that you think you don't deserve me.

I'm just plain folks who got lucky one day in 1968 in Eugene, Oregon.

Love, Carol Beth Haole

My Dear Wife,

It was 31 years ago when we went forth on our odyssey together, when we laid out our plans and began our journey through life no longer as individuals, but as man and wife, a team, a partnership. For 31 years you slept by my side, loved and comforted me, cooked my meals, hugged me and kissed me and supported me whenever I was down. During that time you gave me our children, loved, cared for and nurtured them and raised them into extraordinary people.

I cannot remember a moment when our marriage was not blissful. It is filled with so much joyful memories beginning with learning to make house, buying and refurbishing old furniture, scrounging for household items, throwing dinners for new found friends, traveling through the US of A and touring Europe.

Now when I look back on it, our life together reads like a storybook. It was exciting and passionate, loving and warm and filled with all those things that count for a truly good life.

What got me through a stressful career was your continuing, tender and understanding reminders to me about what really was important, your touches, your warm and supportive eyes, your disinterest in material things, your glow and joy for being a mother to our children.

To this day, I continue to ask myself why you bothered to marry this oriental boy. I am so glad you did.

HAPPY ANNIVERSARY

Your Lover

At the end of one long day, at about midnight, Carol came out of the shower and announced that the day just ended had been our wedding anniversary. My son had been having a party at our house that day, and the day had been filled with preparations and all manner of activity. She and I had been so distracted, we had forgotten. My parents and my children did not remember. Everyone had forgotten. We had not observed that occasion. After 35 years of blissful marriage, I had completely forgotten the celebration of the most important event of my life.

The following morning Carol went to work, and I went to work on the following email searching for atonement from an unpardonable lapse in memory.

Dear Wife,

At the end of our son's party and the end of the day, as you dried yourself, still wet from your bath, you exclaimed with astonishment that the day just ended had been our wedding anniversary. Is it true that our day had gone by without notice or remembrance? How can it be?

In the morning after, my heart still yearned for some whisper of an answer. How could we have forgotten the day we embarked on our greatest adventure?

How can it be? It must be because every day you have been with me has been a soulful vow no less than the vows we took when we wed.

How can it be? It must be because every day after that day of our sacred promises have become days of promises kept.

How can it be? It must be because we have truly become one, that we had achieved the very commandment that on that day the Monsignor had pronounced, and so every day thereafter has been like the first.

It must be because the love you promised you have given, because the gleam in your eyes has delivered the joy that is our children, and thus, every day since that blessed day has been a day as blessed.

It is because every day with you has been like the day we married.

As I said on that first day and have said every day since, and now say again and again as long as breath remains.....I love you.

Your Husband

Dear Husband,

You are right, of course. What is one date in a year of 35 years, when every day is a reaffirmation? You are and always will be the right one for me. Even as you rethink who you are and what you want to do, you are so supportive of everything I do, and your dinners are great too.

We are lucky to have good, healthy kids, but they are also very lucky to have us. Maybe, they should take us out for an anniversary dinner.

I love you.

Carol

What is a husband to do when annual events such as Valentine's Day, Mother's Day and Anniversary come around so often? I mean what do you say or get for a gift? Over the years, she has paid the bills. She has had possession of the check book. She has had the credit cards. She is in total control of all our accounts. What I have is hers. What she has is hers. Whatever she wants she has the means to buy. Despite a long marriage, I have never successfully purchased and gifted items to her of a personal nature that she liked. Instead, I am usually challenged to write her something from my heart, like the note that follows.

Here it is again, dear Wifey, Valentine Day. It is upon us, and I have neither a gift nor chocolates wrapped.

I thought that I might cook you dinner, but then I do that anyway.

I could surprise you by doing the laundry, but then I do that anyway.

So, I planned to vacuum and clean the house, but alas, I do that anyway.

Upon much circumspection, it came to me to give you what all women would die for, but then.....I am already yours.

So I've concluded that since you have everything, no gift could improve upon your happiness, save this greeting, trite as it is....

HAPPY VALENTINE DAY

Your Hubby

Every year, special occasions to celebrate my wife repeat themselves. They seem to come in rapid succession. There is our wedding anniversary, Mother's day, Valentine's Day, the holidays and her birthday. After 38 years, there have been hundreds of such occasions. That would be a lot of cards and a lot of notes. So how does one continue to keep the message fresh and new? How does one say I love you differently every time? To write a note or not, that is the challenge. Pressed with this very dilemma, I wrote the following:

Dear Wifey,

Do not be concerned though in recent days I have been hearing voices.

The one on the left tells me to write a romantic note to you for Valentine's Day.

The one on the right presses the futility of crafting expressions better than Hallmark and the world's greatest poets and writers.

The one on my left responds that it is better that I deliver a note than not. It is better, it says, than that I demonstrate no effort at all.

The voice on the right argues that there are no expressions that mere mortals are capable of that could possibly do justice to my intent, my love and gratitude for you. It persists that the breadth of all my love for you cannot possibly be contained in a note, a memorandum, a book or even a library. It continues that the greatness of my love for you renders dumb the most romantic languages of the world.

I have decided that the right is right ....so I have not written you a note.

Your Hubby

CHAPTER TEN

Joyful Returns

*"Thank you mom for always cheering me up with
one of your corny jokes when I was sad. Thank
you for doing my laundry."*

If it is possible to summarize my feelings about taking in
little strangers, it is that taking them into our homes will reap the
blessings that defy our best attempts to describe. In return,
there is love, and to love there is no equivalent. As a parent you
have the right and license to love them unconditionally and
without restraint. You can tickle them until they can take no
more; toss them in the air until they giggle and squirm; hug them
to pieces for as long and as often as you want; kiss them until
there is not an inch of face left untouched by your lips; take
them in with prideful eyes and not be accused of discourtesy;
take them wherever you want to show them off; shamelessly
boast in public about their successes without disapproval; watch
them with satisfaction as you fill them with contentment; bounce
them on their bed so many times that they cry for mercy; bask in
their attention and their love returned; pull the covers over their
heads after receiving their hugs and kisses; laugh at their

curious responses to novel experiences; rejoice in life again through their living theirs in the love you give them: and, take as much pride and credit as you can steal for their many accomplishments. They are far, far better than Tickle Me Elmo dolls; they respond with goodness to all the goodness you give them. Best of all, they don't need batteries.

If you love them, they will return it. For Christmas 2001, I received a poem created and written by Kelly. In my life as a father there have been numerous such returns from all of my children. This is one of them.

Little Feet and Little Faces
© 2001 by Dr. Kelly B.T. Chang

Do you miss the little feet
Running down the hall to wake you up for
Christmas?
Do you miss the little faces
Bright with anticipation to open up their presents?
Maybe your heart is sad
That your children are grown up and going out
And maybe Christmas just isn't the same
as the times when little ones ran about.
But let me tell you that the joy of Christmas isn't
over.
You've put it in our hearts
You've wrapped it around our lives,
And the happiness we've shared
Over many years and under many trees,
Will live on forever in our memories.
And one day
We'll pass it on to the little feet and little faces

That we've brought into the world.
And while we wait for newborn graces, listen to
your little girl:
I will always be your happy child at Christmas
time.
Because you always make me smile
You still make the house shine.
We will always love to be with you on Christmas
day.
Because your Christmas lights and Christmas
hugs
Will always show us the way.
With many Christmases yet to come,
We'll always love our Christmas home!
So thank you for wrapping Christmas around
Our little feet and little faces.
We hope you'll know how bright and warm
We think your Christmas place is!

To her mother, on April 11, 2001, Erin wrote of her love and appreciation. She handed this quickly written note in an envelope to her mother with instructions that it be opened when she was on the plane returning to me in Hawaii.

Dearest Mom (Head),

You should be on the plane now. I am happy that I
at least got to see you for a short while. I am so blessed
by Jesus that he gave me a mother like you. You are not
only a patient, loyal, loving, caring, giving and
compassionate mother but you are a best friend and
confidante. I always feel that I can talk to you about

*anything in my heart. God gave you a lot of His qualities.
I miss you and Dad (Kevin, Kelly and Max, of course) a
lot. I can't imagine not having you around for the rest of
my life. I don't even like to think about it, but in my heart I
always pray that we will all be together in Heaven with
Jesus some day. Because I pray this, I know God will
answer and that makes me feel better. I owe a lot to you
and Dad for being so good to me. I really believe that I
have the best parents. I just hope this letter shows you
how much I really thank Jesus for you.*

*Thank you mom for always cheering me up with
one of your corny jokes when I was sad. Thank you for
doing my laundry. Thank you for cooking me meals that
went with all my crazy eating habits. Thank you for
driving me to school, theater and church programs.
Thank you for wanting to come to church with me. Thank
you for sending me all your little notes on "Far Side
Calendar" paper along w/ $. Thank you for letting me tell
you my frustrations over the phone w/ you at work. Thank
you for always keeping me level-headed. Thank you for
always being interested in my life and the people in it.
Thank you for always coming into my room to turn the
music down. Thank you for waking me up every morning
for school. Thank you for always tucking me in, correcting
my school papers, seeing my plays more than once,
reading me "Green Eggs and Ham", comforting me when
I had nightmares, trying to answer all my questions,
taking me shopping for bras and underwear, buying me
food, helping me decorate my apartment, believing and
supporting me in my dreams. Thank you for singing all
your unique Irish songs. Thank you for giving practical
and not so practical and rather weird gifts. Thank you for
staying up late with me and handling all my moods.*

Thank you for always being a great host to all my friends. Thank you for feeding me vegetables, V-8 juice, wheat bread and tasteless, but healthy cereal. (: Thank you for helping me to see the bigger picture in all situations. Thank you for always caring about where I was. Thank you for praying with me. Thank you Mom for being all of this and more. I love you with all my heart.

Love, Little Erin (aka Er-head)

P.S. Call me so I know you arrived safely.

Kelly wrote this sweet note to me on my birthday,

Happy Birthday, Dear Dad,

This is just a reminder that you are not old. You have simply added another year of blessing this universe with your presence to your portfolio. You are vastly experienced, but not old. You are wise, enlightened, knowledgeable, seasoned, perfected, fine-tuned, polished, well-practiced, and a master of all that is life, but you are not too old.

*   *   *

Your hair is not gray; it is peppered with wisdom. Your skin is not wrinkled; it is textured with experience. Your back does not ache; it reminds you that you have stood strong for what is right. Your arms are not weaker; they remind you that you have held and protected three tiny babies as they have grown...and boy, have they.

Your memory is not poor; it is rich with family, love and achievements.

No matter how many years you've been on this earth, I am thankful for every one of them. You are one of the best gifts God could ever give me. I pray often that you and I will grow old ... I mean mature and experienced...together. And I pray that you will have many opportunities to be the wonderful grandpa I know you will be---that's way down the road, so you will have more years to become even more wise, mature, experienced and polished.

I love you.

For her mother, Kelly wrote:

If You Only Knew

If you only knew how much your smile brightens my day,

You would use it to hold back the clouds and storms that come our way.

If you only knew how much your embrace sooths my soul,

You would use it to comfort the world of its many sorrows.

If you only knew how happy having you

For my mother has made me.

You would want to be mother to the world.

Even so, I'm glad I have you all to myself.

Happy Mother's Day, mom.

To me Kelly wrote the following:

> *…Thank you, dad, for being so interested in my life…in the way I grew up, in helping me to learn and overcome problems, in providing more than I ever needed, in coming in every night to say good night, say you love me and asking me if I had any questions. Thank you for the special times we got to spend together…helping me move into my apartment, skiing, touring San Francisco, giving me a job in your office, and taking me out to lunch every day, and all the other things you have done to make me feel special and loved. Thank you for all your wise advice. I would often tell people things that you had said, and they would say, "Wow, you have a really wise father." And I'd say, "Yep, I do."*

*   *   *

> *Thank you daddy for working so hard so that I could go to the college I want and study the things I want to. Thank you for keeping yourself healthy, jogging and eating right. I am very thankful that I do not have to worry about yours and mom's health while I'm so far away. Thank you for writing all those email messages that have helped me so much with my autobio. Thank you for being involved in my learning, helping me to improve in my high school Japanese class, working with me on a science*

project, telling me all these things for my paper, discussing all my options for study with me. Thank you for letting me go when it was necessary for me to do things on my own. Thank you for being the loving guide without being a smothering dictator. That is balance that I'm sure most people have difficulty finding...but you did! Thank you for always hugging me and making me feel like a precious little princess.

Ever since she was a toddler, Erin always displayed her ability to project her voice. She filled our house with songs and silly chatter at very high decibels and she almost always seemed unaware that the person she may be talking to was not just closer than earshot of her, but just a whisper away. Anyone within shouting distance would become an unwilling participant in the most private conversation she was having with another. Her voice could be heard by neighbors even across a wide natural gulch behind our house. This natural talent (if indeed it was a talent) presaged her becoming a singer and songwriter.

Erin wrote the following to her mother:

A Mother's Arms

A mother's arms are arms that will hold you all the time.

In times of danger, her arms hold you as protector from a storm.

In times of sadness, her arms hold you like a sponge soaking up all your tears.

In times of happiness, her arms hold you like a cuddly teddy bear.

But most of all, in times of taking the greatest steps in life, her arms hold you like a best friend, never wanting to let go.

She has parlayed this natural ability to project her voice into her singing, and she has written or collaborated with others in writing many beautiful songs celebrating her wedding on a hill, remembering a close friend on a pier, poking fun at her husband's luck to have her, painting the troubled lights in the City of Las Vegas and highlighting love that grows in a garden and blossoms under a tangerine tree. She completed her first music album named after her, her professional name, Elina. She included snippets of her grandfather's singing, the charming little voice of a pretty and lovely niece, and at the end of the CD, she included a hidden track, a song she had written and sung for her mother. All of these touches mirrored the goodness of her heart.

Hands
© 2003 by Erin ("Elina") Wells

Hands, hands that kept me from harm
Hands that held onto my own
Feet, feet that ran to and fro
Feet, that kept up to my own

Mother, faithful friend, helping hand
Constant, open arms to my heart

Mother, if I could love the way you do
Then I'd be a God-sent angel too

You live with a joyful soul
Finding gold and the worth in all
You give, like there's always more
Lending time and an open door

Erin and her husband, Tyrone, both of whom are songwriters, artists and singers, had committed to a long road tour through much of the East Coast, as far north as New Hampshire and as far south as Alabama, Colorado and South Carolina and Florida. This itinerary was displayed on their websites. They were to perform at more than 100 venues from August through December and continuing again in January through March. When I first saw their itinerary, I feared that it would be a grueling, tedious and difficult trip through the winter months often fighting holiday traffic and bad weather and driving through dangerous winter conditions. My mind conjured long tedious miles of rolling pavement, windows rolled up to keep out cold and rain, condensation on windows, the incessant scraping of windshield wipers, the rushing of the car heater and treacherous black ice. Such conditions would challenge the strongest relationships. The worry over it often seemed to hover over me, and even after successfully laying it aside, it would return to me in a quiet moment.

One of my strengths and my weaknesses has always been my analytical mind. I tend to analyze everything I observe. I questioned, for example, why the Mondo grass in our front yard would form mounds and eventually die off. Studying the problem, I realized that the grass propagates by putting out lateral stringers above ground. At the end of these stringers were little plants that would settle into the earth, root and become a new plant, so I reasoned that as the plants crowded together the little plants were suspended in the air and could not set roots into the ground; thus forming mounds. As the little plants grew bigger the root system of the mother plant could no longer support the plants that were not rooted and the plants would eventually die.

Bamboo that was growing in our front yard was constantly topped off by our gardeners so as to form a hedge. I wanted the bamboo to become graceful again; I did not want a bamboo hedge. I cut the bamboo down to the ground, but for years thereafter, as the bamboo grew back it would not resume its natural graceful form; it got bushy at the top just as it did when it was a hedge. Apparently, it had some form of memory of being bushy. Over the years, that memory seemed to dissipate and the bamboo went back to its natural shape. Since it had been cut down to the ground, where was the memory, I wondered. It had to be somewhere in the root system, but where? How was its prior shape retained? Since it finally resumed its natural shape, it must have had a memory of what it should be, but how? It suggests that man can train the bamboo to act unnaturally as is done with bonsai plants. Are all plants trainable? How long does this retentive power last before resuming its natural shape?

Questioning enables me to see problems even before they develop. If I want, for example, to drive somewhere and I am familiar with the area, in my mind's eye I can see my trip, every turn, every intersection, likely traffic delays, all the way to the parking space where I will park. Problems need to be confronted and solved. Problems should not be allowed to fester. Because I have an active analytical mind, I usually am quick to come up with solutions or answers. I do not always know the correct answers or even the right solutions, but I usually know the questions. The questions are like road maps that guide me to within striking distance of an answer, and it becomes so clear to me so quickly that I would be busting with the need to tell someone.

In the context of business or in the practice of law, these abilities are, more often than not, strengths. In the context of human relations, these strengths can be weaknesses. Impatience and irritability are the sad result. I am easily bored with frivolous matters and impatient with what I perceive as dalliance, procrastination or ineptitude. I am busting with the need to relieve my mind of my thoughts. I am, thus, disposed to giving advice and counsel, requested or not. I usually try mightily not to do this when my advice is not welcomed. I was more predisposed to doing this with my children even when they grew up, matured and moved out of the house. If I saw that they were at risk, I felt an obligation to insert my opinions. If I thought that they were about to take a step off the edge of a cliff, I believed it was my obligation to shout out. Moreover, I loved them so much, that I could not endure the image my mind would conjure of any resulting disaster. After my opinions were made known, however, wisdom usually restrained me from pressing the matter further. So it was when I foresaw the tedium, difficulties and danger of Tyrone and Erin's long road tour.

I remembered that when Carol and I would take long road trips we would play word games to moderate the boredom Hangman was one of them, and Password was another. We would do this usually at the behest of my loving companion and wife. So, I devised some similar way of distracting them from the boredom of traveling over hundreds of miles of roads. I sent them a copy of Kelly's poem, "Little Feet and Little Faces", and challenged them to turn it into a song to sing it to me on

Christmas. I had sent it via email and I had not received a response, not even an acknowledgement.

Over time, I forgot all about that request. I did not think much about it because making that suggestion, in and of itself, was effective in allaying my own anxieties. Sending that proposal to them succeeded in relieving me of my nagging fear. Moreover, as their tour progressed it just seemed to me that Tyrone was doing all he could to minimize the adverse effects of such a long road tour, including taking many breaks from the tedium and surprising his wife with the company of a dear friend and sister midway through their tour. He is a thoughtful, sensitive, loving and exceptional husband and son-in law. Erin's usual good judgment of people had found him out and brought him home to all of us to enrich our family.

Christmas day 2006 was a great Christmas. My entire family was around the tree that Christmas morning. I could not have asked for more than that we were all together on that joyful day. As was traditional in our family, we opened gifts in turn together, talked about what we had received, laughed, shared meals, sentiments and conversation. We did this throughout the morning. After the last gift under the tree had been opened and it appeared that there was nothing else there, Kelly said, "Dad, there is something under the tree." I looked under the tree and saw nothing, but when asked to look again, I retrieved an envelope that was addressed to "Daddy". Still unsuspecting, I opened the envelope and found two pages of what appeared to be a song by Kelly, Tyrone and Erin, entitled, "Little Feet and Little Faces." The lyrics had been based, in part, on Kelly's poem. The music chords were clearly designated. The memory of my request made months ago came rushing back. As I was beginning to take all of it in and find the words to react, Tyrone quickly left the room to retrieve his guitar. He returned just as quickly and slipped by his wife's side on the living room sofa in front of our Christmas tree. Erin began by singing to the A chord picked and strummed by Tyrone. She was accompanied by Tyrone's soft, sweet, melodioius voice.

Little Feet and Little Faces
© 2006 by Kelly Chang, Erin ("Elina") and Tyrone Wells

*Little feet quickly running up and down the stairs
Little faces peeking down to see the presents there
As the gifts were opened up, you made sure joy was shared. What we will remember Dad is just how much you cared*

*Little feet and little faces long grown up and gone.
Echo in your memory like an old time Christmas song
If your heart grows heavy Daddy, as time slips away. I hope you know the love you shared lives on in me today*

Someday soon on Christmas, I'll give what you gave me

To the little feet and little faces that will be your legacy

*Christmas Eve around the fire we sang those Christmas songs
You were always making sure that we would sing along*

Decorations, Christmas lights and stockings on the stairs

Storytelling, family time, you were always there

*Little feet and little faces long grown up and gone
Echo in your memory like an old time Christmas song*

If your heart grows heavy Daddy, as time slips away

I hope you know the love you shared lives on in me today

Someday soon on Christmas, I'll give what you gave me

To the little feet and little faces that will be your legacy

*Someday soon on Christmas, I'll give what you gave me
To the little feet and little faces that will be your legacy*

Doing everything I could to maintain my composure, I reached far within myself to muster the strength I did not know I had to hold back the tears that I thought would be unbecoming a father. This was made more difficult in the sight of tears rushing down Erin's cheeks and her attempts to hold the notes while resisting the tears welling in her throat. Added to this overwhelming moment were all the tears of my beloved wife sitting across from me. The tenderness of the song, the sweetness of Erin's presentation and the sincerity of Tyrone's accompaniment brought home so forcefully the priceless blessing of the moment. As they sang the song they had labored secretly to create and to practice, and as each word and note vanished past my hearing and rested in my heart, something within me quietly, but futilely, revolted against the passing of that Christmas day. My heart whispered a prayer that we would all be frozen in that moment.

I had made a half-hearted attempt to ward off the dangers of the road for them, a desperate attempt to relieve a father's fears, and they had converted it into the best Christmas present I had ever received. It had already been a Christmas full of happiness, and at the second before I opened the envelope, I had thought that more joy was not possible to be borne by a human heart. Kelly, Tyrone and Erin's gift of song proved me wrong. That blessed Christmas of 2006 had all been in the making when Carol and I had accepted tiny little strangers into our home, and one of them brought home a very good, talented and generous soul named Tyrone, our much loved son-in-law.

It is my hope that whenever "Little Feet and Little Faces" is performed that it will be dedicated to all good fathers who have taken little strangers, their little feet and little faces, into their homes and into their hearts.

CHAPTER ELEVEN

Christmases Past

"When I hug you to say I love you and wish you a safe trip, though my arms are around you, I cannot hold you."

Christmas in our family was always a special time and we would do it up big. It was the one time that my usually frugal self would be restrained and I would loosen my grip on my wallet. Whenever I went shopping for them I would be motivated by the surprise and joy that I imagined their gifts would bring to their faces. Whenever I would think that I had purchased enough gifts for them, I would worry that each of them would not have as many as the other to open. When they were small I would literally race through the aisles of a toy store with a cart, my wallet and a big smile on my face. As they grew away from toys, I had to be more thoughtful and cautious about what I purchased. Very soon it became apparent to me that the stress of guessing what colors, sizes, styles and clothing would please them was taking the fun out of shopping for gifts. So, when they were much older, we asked them to write letters to Santa telling Santa precisely what they wanted. I would, of course, be the one to mail the letters to Santa.

As they grew older they repudiated, for awhile, the notion that Santa was fictitious, in part, probably because it was profitable and, in part, probably because they wanted to humor their dad who got so much enjoyment out of this seasonal custom. So, they continued to write these letters to Santa. Soon the pages grew from one to a few. Soon the items asked for began to grow and the specifications for each item became more precise. At times, the letters would even tell Santa the type and style of clothing, the size, the color and the accessories that went with it.

Dear Santa,

How are you? I'm great. What I want for Christmas is:

The biggest size of caboodle (in black and white or in another color)

The hair organizer caboodle (in black and white)

A gift certificate from Contempo Casuals, Wet Seal and Wild Flowers, plus clothes and accessories from there: earrings, designer toothbrush, a big metal cross on a metal chain, charm bracelet, big charms on necklaces. A Champagne bubble bath, oil balls from Liberty House

A good, good walkman, Sony

Money

A black purse the kind with the long strap and not big and bulky, a small black purse. You can ask my mom what kind of purse.

A subscription to Teen Magazine.

          *   *   *

Love, Erin

Dear Santa,

          *   *   *

I told my dad that gift certificates are best, but clothes with their receipts are just the same, and more fun to open. If I don't like it or it doesn't fit, I can trade it for something else. My favorite stores are Wildflowers, Wet Seal, and Hartfield's.

Christmas things

I'd still like a computer with laser printer, but if you can't afford it, I understand.

A gift certificate for Coverlook (sort of like Model You) that I can use before the Junior Prom.

I think that's it. I hope you have a great Christmas.

Love, Kelly

In some cases, these letters to Santa even told Santa what stores and even what shelves these items were being offered on. Mercenary? Commercial? Yes, to both. But, it made my search for the appropriate gift much less stressful and much more pleasant, and everyone got what he or she wanted, and dad still got to hold onto the fantasy that they believed in Santa

Claus just a little while longer. Besides, they had grown into that phase of their lives when pragmatism had begun to assert itself. If anything, the letters to Santa were practical, and what really became practical was the sad and inevitable acceptance, that they really did not believe in Santa. Another wonderful phase in my life had come to an end.

After putting our children to bed on Christmas Eve, Carol and I would get ourselves into high gear. Despite the exhaustion of the day and the lateness of the hour, we were energized by the images of their smiles and the sound of their laughter, their joy and the hugs that would be ours on Christmas morning. Before going to bed the children had put the milk and cookies out for Santa, so we had to make sure that the milk was drunk and the cookies consumed; it would have disturbed them if they woke up to find evidence of an ungrateful Santa. Santa would also have to respond to the notes they had set out for him. Presents from Santa were retrieved from their hiding places, put under the tree and stuffed into stockings that had been specially knitted by their grandmother, or as she liked to be called, Grand Nan.

When our children noticed that the gifts from Santa were wrapped with the same gift paper that we used on other gifts under our tree, we had to wrap Santa's gifts to them with special and different gift paper and ribbon. The gift paper and the ribbons destined to wrap gifts to them from Santa were concealed from them in the weeks leading up to Christmas.

When I was a child, I remember that on Christmas morning we would go through all of our gifts in half an hour. It was the built-up anticipation and the excitement that I could not restrain; I had to know what was contained under all those wrappings and ribbons and I had to know right away. I ripped through anything that bore my name and I paid very little attention to whom it was from. In half an hour, every gift under the tree had been opened and all that remained were the boxes, used and torn gift wrappings and ribbons piled around the tree. In one half hour, the expectation, the surprise and the joy of opening gifts were gone. When I had our family, we were determined to change that custom.

In our home on Christmas morning, opening gifts under the tree was practically an all-day affair interrupted only by breakfast and lunch and sometimes even dinner. We would all sit around the tree, put a fire in the fireplace, put on the Christmas music, and turn on the Christmas lights in the room and on the tree. Until the mood was set, and all the family was gathered around the tree, not one gift was allowed to be opened. Everyone had to be sitting in a cozy circle by the tree before gifts could be unwrapped. The first, next and last gift would not be opened until it was approved. Everyone was required to watch as one of us opened a gift. Everyone would share the surprise and joy that that gift brought. Everyone had to participate in watching that person's "happiness." If it were a dress, she would hold it up for all to see, and at times, she would even put it on and model it to everyone's delight. If it were a toy truck, he would take it out of the box, insert the batteries and drive it around the room for all to admire. Until this was done, the next gift would not be opened. This custom heightened and sustained expectation (and extended a father's joy at watching that expectation soar in their little faces) and generated a lot of laughter, banter, familial conversation, hugs and kisses.

The whole process would sometimes extend up to Christmas dinner when our guests began to arrive. Even as they were arriving, we would be picking up the wrapping paper and used ribbons, setting aside the yet-unopened gifts for a later time and tidying around the tree for the party.

As they grew into adults, the pretense of Santa Claus that had brought so much joy to our family during the Christmas holidays became unseemly, and to their dad's dismay, the letters to Santa stopped. As young adults attending college, what they needed more than anything else was money. Writing them a check was not as much fun in the unwrapping and it was without all the merriment, excitement and expectation of Christmas gifts under the tree. I was deeply saddened by these changes, but we maintained as much of the custom as was possible. We tried to make sure there were some gifts that still could be placed under the tree and unwrapped Christmas morning, but there was no denying the melancholy that the absence of little feet and little faces and the ebb of a cherished family tradition brought to the Christmas season.

Dear Children,

This is the dress, the blouse, the trousers, the shirt, the skirt, the sweater and other personal items that had we selected would have been too small, too large, the wrong color, the incorrect texture, too tasteless, the wrong match,...

This is in place of having to save sales receipts and empty boxes, and your having to drag them in large plastic bags to exchange items purchased with the best of intentions, but without the perceptivity to know your thoughts and desires.

This is for our wish that you will obtain more of what you want more cheaply from the abundance of post Christmas sales.

This is for our wish that you will be able to get what you want at the right time, at the right place and with or for the right person.

Although it may seem that loving thought was not devoted to the making of this gift, it is not true. Now at this time when you are young adults, it is the gift that truly allows you to fill your most urgent needs rather than the unconscious needs of the donor. There may be bills that need to be paid, restaurants that need trying, movies that need to be seen, itches that need scratching and a host of thousands of other possible desires that need satisfaction. Each dollar was hard earned and worked for, and each is lovingly given by parents who are very proud of each and all of their children.

So now, I have arrived at that time when all my children are grown and out of the house. I am asked to and must accept this change with grace and courage just as I must with all the other natural changes of life. I must let them go to live the lives we sacrificed for and strived to give them.

I stood by you awkwardly and silently, knowing the passing minutes brought you closer to boarding the plane that would take you away. There I was the trial attorney, the lawyer, the advocate, too depressed and sad to find the words. Watching you leave is such a painful experience. It is one, I guess, I will never get used to.

Perhaps, it is the anguish of all fathers, a suffering to moderate the joy of having raised our sons and daughters. Our children, of course, are not our property. We borrow them for only a little while.

There is emptiness, now, in our four-bedroom and three-bath two story house. There are just two of us to fill this house. Three bedrooms are empty and seldom visited. The tubs, basins and faucets in one of them remain clean, dry and shiny but for a film of settled dust. The bed covers have not been disturbed for months. Every empty corner of these rooms, once filled with so much life, tears and laughter, are laden with a heavy melancholy.

First you were here and too soon you are gone, but you will be back again, and it is the expectation of your return that makes your departure bearable.

When I hug you to say I love you and wish you a safe trip, though my arms are around you, I cannot hold you. No one can hold you down for you must fly away, not so you can leave, but so you can seek, explore, marvel at life and relish new experiences. In order to go you must leave. In order to explore, to seek, to grow, you must depart. For every step forward there is a step away in order to grow, there must be sorrow. It is the expectation of the return that makes the sorrow pass and makes what is ahead more exciting. I will see you at Christmas time.

Now, even before Thanksgiving, I set up a 9-foot artificial tree where on past holidays stood taller authentic noble firs around which little children once sat in awe, with bright-colored lights reflected in their eyes. Plastic bags, ragged from age and use, and strands of tree lights, some blue, some red, orange and green and some white, are strewn on the floor, the sofa and chairs, ready to be tested and set up. Karen Carpenter sings my favorite carols, "Merry Christmas, darling...." Her sweet notes fill the house and bring memories of the many years when they competed with the romp and laughter of children. I am alone in the company only of her voice. The house is empty. My wife is gone to work and no other heart beats here but mine. There is no sound but that that I make. There is not a whisper or wish in this house, save the utterances in my heart. There is no one to assist, no one to share the cheer and merriment that come with the season. There is just me in a large living room, under a soaring cathedral ceiling, setting up the tree and testing the lights. Funny, I never noticed how much space there was in this living room. The loneliness seems almost to be holding up the ceiling and pushing out through the windows. It is oppressive. I feel more detached from, than involved in, the decorating. It must be like how store clerks must feel when forced by their bosses to decorate storefronts. "Who will admire the tree?" I wondered. "Who will sing along with me?" Where are those little eyes that once reflected the lights and lit my heart? I can fill the spaces with familiar old things disinterred from the attic, but there are no little feet and little faces, just a lot of cold, once-lively spaces.

When you were just a little girl, I would, after a bout of rolling around with you and tickling you until you begged for breath, pause to stare into those big brown eyes for what seemed like hours..., and in the depth of those big eyes, I would lose myself and all my troubles. That is how you got your name "Big Eyes." Your big round face would seem to wonder what the meaning was for my fixed and intrusive gaze, but undaunted, you would stare right back at me defiantly as if to say, "...and so there."

An American poet wrote "Stopping by Woods on a Snowy Evening" and in it he said about a rider on a horse that stared into the woods, "...but I have miles and miles to go before I sleep..." Your eyes were like the woods, but now I stare at the fire in the fireplace, and it is you that have miles and miles to go before you sleep.

For it is not possible anymore for me to hold those eyes with my gaze. Those eyes now wander. They are restless and on the go, there is not time for letting a father stare too long into them. There are things to see with those eyes. There are places to take those eyes. There are many joys, sorrows, happiness and disappointments for those eyes to behold. There is your life to live and not much time to let a father's longing lips linger anymore on soft dimpled cheeks. It is a change that saddens me, for now as I move into the shadows you must step forward into the lights of the stage. My time for the big play has faded. Your time to shine is here.

Familiar old tree ornaments have become remembrances of little feet that no longer run, skip and jump around in exuberance and excitement. There are no cherubic faces looking with unbridled expectation and uncontainable

excitement at the approaching Christmas day. These familiar
ornaments are memories of Santa Claus laps, family laughter,
sheepish grins, joyful faces, wrapped surprises, moist kisses,
lingering hugs and torn ribbon and Christmas paper strewn all
over beneath the tree. Here are pictures of my children in much
earlier days. Added last Christmas and again this Christmas,
hanging from a bough, is the picture of our talented son-in-law.
Here is one made by beloved little hands in grammar school.
Time has faded it. Here is another made by the same little
hands in the shine of their mother's love. The store-purchased
ornaments are dull next to those made by little hands. There is
so much joy and sadness in all of them.

*Soooo...then why do I always think of you as my
little Big Eyes? It is probably too simple to say that it is
just the way it is. Maybe fathers hold to their fantasy to
preserve ourselves. Perhaps, it can be explained by the
awful sadness that overtook me once as I watched on
television a fierce, growling mother bear chase away her
confused, crying and despondent cub whose time it was
to live by itself. It made me so sad, and every time I
thought of it my sadness became even more profound. I
don't want to chase you away. I can't do it. So instead, I
pretend that you are still with me. Still, I know that you
are not. It helps me to cope with the rudeness of this
change.*

Christmas is a glorious seasonal snapshot of life,
sadness and joy wrapped together in every corner. So when joy
comes knocking, no matter what the season, embrace it. As we
choose to sweeten a drink too sour to our taste, the joy we are

given helps sweeten our life. As we choose to drink it, sour or sweet, how we live our life is how we choose to live it. Little strangers can be the sweetener of life, if we let them in.

Now the little faces and little feet are gone. Now all those wonderful Christmases are memories. I am glad to have the memories, but I must admit to being selfish enough to want even more. I cannot revisit the past Christmases; I cannot have back their little voices singing songs from *The Little Mermaid*; I cannot sit back as I used to and watch my son put on his puppet shows and my daughters dance with their Little Strawberry Shortcake masks on. I cannot put them to bed and whisper softly to them and push down on their heads to slow their growing, and, most of all, I cannot have them sit still to listen to a father's hopes and prayers for them. No more. Those years are gone. Life's promises fast become memories before we can even begin to understand that they do. It was dreams and expectations that first drove us; now it is memories that sustain us. I am grateful for the memories, but I know that there was a time when I really had it good.

Our first to be married was our youngest daughter, Erin. She and her husband live in California and for the first few years of their marriage, they have always returned to Hawaii to spend Christmas with us. One year in October, Erin flew in to Hawaii from California for the principle purpose of assisting with and attending a birthday celebration that was being planned for her good friend, Tisha. She stayed most of that time at Tisha's house. Carol and I were invited over for dinner. In the living room, the conversation somehow turned to Erin's expected return trip to Hawaii in a couple months for the Christmas season and how much we were looking forward to that event. Erin happened into the living room when the conversation was taking place. Without a segue, she blurted, "Dad, you cannot expect us at every Christmas season. We may decide to spend it with others."

At the time this was said, Carol was in the kitchen and so was Tisha. Upon hearing this, Tisha, gasped and said, "Uh, oh…"

This was undoubtedly the beginning of her softening up her father. Erin was preparing me for the time when she and Tyrone would not be spending Christmas with us. It was, however, a time I knew was coming, but a time I dreaded. I was not surprised, for no father can nor should expect that his grown children will always be with him at Christmas time. They have new lives and new families and soon they must invite strangers into their homes and begin their own families and traditions. It was apparent to me, however, that Erin was anxious about that moment and that she had been expressing her concerns to her best friend, Tisha, about how she was going to do this without doing too much damage to her father.

That she worried and fretted evidences a caring and loving heart, a daughter's heart. For that I am grateful. I ask her not to let her heart be troubled. For when that time comes, I promise to accept it with grace and without "pouting." I may not have the stout heart of a mother bear, but it will be as if I hugged her and whispered in her ear-- as I did when I danced at her wedding-- "I love you."

We see as our next obligation to you to keep the home fires burning. Your home will always be here. Here you will get the love and support and comfort you may need as you go on your forays out into the world. This will always be your refuge, your sanctuary, your safe harbor.

The beacon will always shine to guide your way back when you are lost. At this inn, there is a permanent place for you. You can never be turned away. We, of course, cannot promise you that you will always be happy, but we can promise you this: You will never be left out in the cold without shelter from the elements; you will never starve and you'll always have clothing, and as long as we live, we will love and cherish you.

CHAPTER TWELVE

And Then They Are Gone

"O Ireland. What nameless, restive spirits are these that float about your countryside and mercilessly haunt and lure the soul?"

With our children out of the house, Carol and I have been doing some traveling. We went to China and to Ireland. In Ireland, we stayed in a white-washed cabin with a thatch roof, nestled in the hills of Connemara close to the Quiet Man Bridge just outside of Oughterard. There we burned turf in a large fireplace, walked the area around the cabin and toured Galway, The Burren, the Cliffs of Moher and Connemara. While in Ireland, there was a mood that had come over me and stayed with me even upon my return. I was moved to write the following:

Whispers in Connemara

O, listen… listen to the whistling, whiffing, softly whispering breezes; the swishing of the waves of sweet, pungent grass pirouetting over gentle, sinuous hills where lonely shepherds shook off the cold blast over northern seas; the falling, splashing, cold spring waters rushing, tripping along on their baptismal mission; the distant, plaintive bleat, bleat, bleating of wayward sheep. But loudly more is the tight embrace of jealous solitude, a nagging, yet soothing peacefulness. It is the chill of the air, the deserted white-washed cottage in the glen, the fluttering of birds from blade to blade as from soul to soul their calls and melodies. It is thousands of furtive, eager whispers wafting in the hills of Ireland, songful messages mournful, haunting notes. There is a peace and beauty and dreadful sadness all at once in them, like that in the tear-filled and beauteous eyes of a mother's sorrow. Theirs are the wailful voices of great suffering, surrender and survival. They tattle about angry ships, martyrdom, birth and burial, battlements and destruction. They acquit the endless ranks of archival walls that like a net keep captive secrets in the earth. They speak of hope, hope lost and hope resurrected. They are voices of lament, of regret, so sad and woeful that they prick the heart like the unrelenting, sorrowful droning of the Irish bagpipes, but everywhere, and like a balm, there is that all-consuming beauty.

O Ireland. What nameless, restive spirits are these that float about your countryside and mercilessly haunt and lure the soul?

We have been married for more than 40 years at the time of this writing. Every night in bed, I kiss her hand and her lips and tell her I love her. We have raised three children. Every night she is lying at my side. In the middle of the night, if I awake and hear her breathing and moving next to me, I am filled with immense satisfaction. Yet, it is true that we continue to discover more about each other. Our first trip to Ireland was no exception.

Carol had heard about a man who shared the same name as her father who had passed just some three years after our wedding. She insisted that we go to visit this perfect stranger. It was and is my character that if ever it is proposed that we do something, I need to be satisfied that the effort makes sense, that it will be worthwhile. Without explanation, she insisted that we see this man. We did not know him. We had never met him. He was a total stranger. The only apparent reason for our visiting him was because he had the same name as her father. She offered no other reason. As it turned out, he lived within walking distance of Bunratty Castle where we had been visiting. Carol was determined to see him. She had to see him. She wanted to see him. She was driven to see him. He was less than a mile away and we had to slog through mud, puddles of water and wet pavement through an Irish drizzle to wend our way through back streets to this person's house. I could not understand why we were doing this, and although I followed, I complained all the way. When we finally arrived at his house, she knocked on the door. I was embarrassed and kept a distance behind her. When he responded to her knock and opened the door she introduced herself. Suddenly, I could hear her voice cracking, and I could hear her struggling with her emotions. When she turned around, I could see the tears welling in her eyes and dripping down her cheeks blending with the rain. All of this was being exhibited to an absolute stranger. All of this was being displayed to an astounded and chastened husband who had no idea until that very moment the depth of meaning this meeting with an absolute stranger had for her, all because he had the same name as her father.

When I married Carol, I was looking forward to the joy that would come with extending my family to include hers. I wanted her parents to become close to mine, and I had hoped that their experiences with the beauty and culture of Hawaii would enrich their lives. I wanted to get to know them better and I wanted to show off to them my pride in loving and caring for their daughter.

Although her father was very ill, there was still much hope because of a pending kidney transplant. In times of such grave danger when so little can be done, hope was all that enabled us to continue with our lives during his illness. Hope was a sanctuary in which we sought to relieve our minds of the terrible worry of impending loss.

When he was ill and hospitalized, we visited him. It was then that Carol told him that she was carrying his grandchild. As he lay ill in that hospital bed I could only imagine how much he wanted to hang on so that he could see his grandson. It would, we hoped, provide an added incentive to get him through his debilitating disease.

It was in the middle of the night when we were awakened by a call from Carol's mother telling us of his passing. I was first to answer the phone and I was crushed by the news. Carol was pregnant with Kevin at the time and her mother insisted that Carol not be put through the mournfulness and sadness of the funeral service. At the time, it seemed that Carol was strong and stoic in the face of her devastating loss. Maybe, it was because she was carrying Kevin, and a mother with child is naturally protective of her child's health and well-being. Whatever it was, there was obviously a depth of feeling that she never shared with me concerning the loss of her father. It took many decades of marriage for me to discover it.

The sudden burst of tears before a total stranger under the rain clouds of Ireland astounded me. I was reminded that there is much more to reason and motivation than can be perceived or explained, and that at times it is best to just go along. I was reminded that there is still so much to learn about this woman who had been my loving, constant companion for most of my life.

We spent the last eight days of our Ireland trip in Dublin, an old, historic city full of contrasts, and of youthfulness, vibrancy and energy. Everywhere in the city were signs of economic prosperity.

Ireland 2002

Much is happening in the city of Dublin. Pubs are full and Guinness flows freely and abundantly. Visitors from all over the world regale the revival. Upon worn and old cobblestones where venerated figures once walked, throngs of spending youth flood into shops, pubs, stores and restaurants and close them down long after the tenacious summer days have surrendered up their light. On those old stone slabs, tired bricks and gray curbs, many thousands of feet shuffle and scrape, trip, walk, dance, evade and hustle throughout the crowded streets as shadows in the night. From eager hands, euros pass over spigots and bars, and cash registers ring. There are smiles all around, laughing, loving, joy, music and singing, and amidst all of this, in this ancient city, the ringing of cellular phones. The music plays on beyond the midnight hour, and young women and men continue to toast away the stresses left behind. Artisans, peddlers and showmen exhibit their wares in the malls and squares. The Temple Bar teems with people, and sleep comes only grudgingly to the banks of the Liffey River. Dublin is alive. It spites the musty, old-but-beautiful cathedrals, the remarkable classical and Gothic architecture, Trinity College in stern attention at the center of the city, and the venerable cold, gray and immovable stones of Ireland's history. Where the dead still haunt these unfeeling stones, the warmth, vigor and frivolity of life plays on. Instructive spirits of the past take heed for here come the present and the future, bursting forth with life.

The rolling pastoral hills of the country are not free from this, for on their narrow dangerous curves, scores of tourists wend their way. The medieval banquets of the now-restored Bunratty Castle brim with visitors, and newly built "car parks" are now overwhelmed with large, smoking buses. The sweet smell of mead, a drink come back from a time gone by, rises from the cooking vats and fills the air where the castle once stood in defiance of invading tribes and raping, pillaging hordes. Now it is invaded by visitors armed with euros and a hunger to hear the castle's stories of destruction and restoration, the story of man's insults to charity and mercy. The cab drivers at Shannon Airport pick up and shuttle their charges who wear amazed, cautious and hopeful looks. The colorful pubs, once solitary in charming rural villages now share their song and drinks with visitors from nations that once launched angry men and hostile ships. The children of old enemies now enliven this stony island promising that the blight will not again set down its awful roots. Though tinged with uneasiness, there is hope and expectation everywhere, even in the thatched cottages of the numerous farms and charming villages. The bed-and

*breakfast signs replace in number the sheep that graze
on the abundant grass that carpet round mountains and
soulful valleys, and the mournful, windswept hills.*

*Old Ireland, prosperity has come. O, poor Ireland,
prosperity has come.*

Some years after our first Ireland trip, I learned that Carol
had wistfully told Erin that it was her hope to return, but this time
with the entire family. When any statement seeming to have the
hint of a promise is made to Erin, even off-handedly, it becomes
a promise that must be kept. The slightest suggestion that
would be of some benefit to Erin, dropped however casually,
because of her persistent nature, will not be allowed to languish
and die. Erin is a shaker and doer, and she does not allow
opportunities to come knocking without inviting them in, closing
the door and barring escape. At every opportunity, she brought
up the subject as though to keep the fire burning with the fuel of
her expectation. Woe to those who do not remember Erin's
persistence.

Taking the entire family to Ireland, needless to say, was
an expensive proposition. My first reaction was to ignore the
idea of it, but when it became clear to me that Carol sincerely
wanted to do this, the frugal part of my nature fell silent as I
allowed myself to imagine how it would bring us all together and
strengthen our family through a common and shared
experience. It was unusual for Carol to want something so
badly, for she is customarily pleased and content with her life,
and she seldom ever expresses wanting to do anything that
involves such an expense. After we married, she steeped
herself in my family culture and had to cope with being uprooted
from the life she was used to in Oregon. She did it with a joyful

heart and without the slightest complaint, so now it was my turn to recognize this with gratitude by going along with her understandable desire to show off the culture of her Irish side. It was, after all, an important and significant part of my children and my wife. Why not? As I allowed my mind to explore all the pleasant possibilities of such a family affair I grew excited and set about planning our trip and making all the necessary arrangements. It was like going through the toy store to buy gifts months before Christmas. I was able to live through that memorable experience all over again.

Our trip began with all of us meeting at Tyrone and Erin's beautiful new home in Chino, California, where we celebrated and enjoyed their spacious house and regaled ourselves in each other's company. From there we flew to Shannon, Ireland, where we rented a GPS and a right-handed van that ran on diesel. We loaded it with our travel weary bodies, our baggage and our burgeoning excitement. After a little initial nervousness driving on the wrong side of the street, Kevin quickly grew accustomed to driving on the streets of Ireland.

On our first night in Ireland, we stayed in Bunratty at the Foxwald Bed and Breakfast owned by the man who shared the same name as Carol's father, the man who was surprised one rainy day with a tearful visitor. We toured Bunratty Castle and folk park and spent two consecutive nights at Durty Nelly's, a pub across from the castle, where we dined and listened to and sang with the crowd and with two talented, graying codgers whose gentle, wizened faces were carved with the history and craggy coastlines of their country. The more ample one held his accordion as though he held an Irish lassie in a tender embrace. With his eyes nearly closed, his spirit seemed to drift in and out of Durty Nelly's as he crooned and occasionally sipped from the tall glasses of Guinness pushed at him by an appreciative audience. Whenever there was a respite, he would open his eyes wider, and let out, in his charming way, a humorous proverb or joke. He would do this in a soft, unpretentious voice in the din of the pub without any regard to whether others heard him or not, and most did not. But I did, for I sat just a few feet from him, and it was as though I was having a privileged private audience with him amidst all the carousing customers. I was won over by his gentleness and unassuming manner, and the humor and charm which seemed to roll off his lips so freely as though it came from an inexhaustible reserve. The other, who was taller and slender, wore a light gray hat as he stooped over his piano with his hands sometimes haltingly playing over the ivory keys while enjoying the mood of the happy songsters prompting his memory of old songs. As they played their instruments, they sang familiar and unfamiliar Irish tunes, and to our surprise, old but well-known songs born and bred in America. As they sang and played, I savored the notion that I had at long last uncovered the famed rich humor, earnest wit, friendliness and joviality of spirit that had been my image of the Irish people, something I had longed to find as I had searched Irish faces during my visits.

In the morning before we left Bunratty, Kevin, Erin and Tyrone sang for our host and hostess, and Kelly performed a hula to Kevin's ukulele and voice. I thanked our host for his hospitality and I thanked him too for the kind and understanding manner he received my tearful wife on that rainy Irish day. After embracing and shaking the hands of our new-found Irish friends, we went up to the city of Galway where we stayed at the Sea Breeze Inn Bed and Breakfast overlooking Galway Bay. The precipitating cold Irish sunshine chased us into the warmth and dryness of a playhouse on the first evening of our stay. There, we laughed uproariously at a romping, fast-paced comedic play, and afterwards, we filled ourselves with drinks and fish and chips before taking cabs back to our bed and breakfast. In the morning before our departure from Galway, Tyrone sang his "Sea Breeze" song to the proprietor of the inn that shared the name and to appreciating guests who happened to drop by. Kelly's graceful hula captivated our host who thought Kelly to be very sexy, and who, in a stolen moment, made a point of telling her so.

We wended our way to Doolin, the Cliffs of Moher, and drove down through Ennis and down to Adare. From Adare, we drove to Killarney and stayed for two nights at a delightful two-century-old manor house overlooking Killarney Lake, at the gateway to Killarney National Park. We circumnavigated the Ring of Kerry, meandered around woodsy lakes, parks and gardens, and toasted at sunsets in downtown Killarney pubs.

Our next visit was to the charming village of Kinsale with its quaint, colorful buildings climbing the hill as though in competition to claim the best perspective of picturesque Kinsale harbor. The bay was speckled with colorful fishing boats and ringed with pubs and restaurants. On the evening of our arrival, we walked around the bay admiring the quaint establishments, boats and gardens. We dined at a cozy restaurant off the harbor and enjoyed the music from the live band at the bar.

On the morning of the next day, we again sang and danced, but this time for our host and hostess in Kinsale, before leaving for Cork and going up to Kilkenny and then Carlow where we stayed the night in a 200-year old mansion of a farmhouse on a sprawling farm. We slept in antique canopied beds, huffed up long winding, spindled staircases, and dined on a specially prepared Irish meal that included lettuce soup. We ate in the glow of candle light, in a large dining room with high ceiling and old cherry wood furnishings. We ended the evening in a comfortable and spacious living room before a crackling fireplace, singing and dancing for Paddy and Maureen, our host and hostess, who smiled and applauded their approval. The evening closed with us reluctantly dragging ourselves up the long stairs to our large rooms from which we had beautiful views of the rolling green hills through tall windows with old-fashioned wooden shutters. The next morning, after filling ourselves with the typical Irish breakfast offerings and after meeting the horses in the nearby fields, we said our final farewell.

We jumped back into our van and drove north toward Dublin where we visited the museums and downed that famous black, bitter brew in its birthplace, the Guinness Brewery. We cruised the city in open double decked buses and were drenched to the bone again by that omnipresent Irish mist. We walked the malls among the locals and tourists, became acquainted with the ghosts and spirits of the city and learned the origins of such sayings as "Saved by the bell", chuckled at jugglers and other buskers on the malls, toured the prisons where famed revolutionaries gave their lives for their cause, and stuck our fingers in bullet holes in the columns of the old main post office on O'Connell Street where they had taken their last stand. We went to a performance by the Dubliners, who sang "Happy Birthday" to Carol, and we dined and drank in the frivolity of the pubs at Temple Bar several evenings. In the city of Dublin, there was never a dull day or night.

Ireland and what it had to offer was fine and enjoyable. For Carol and me, much of it was familiar on our second visit, but it could have been China or Africa, or anywhere, as long as we were together as a family. It was the connection we made with our hosts at the bed and breakfasts, and it was the pride in our family's entertaining them that were most enjoyable. For Carol and me, our enjoyment was in observing our family's enjoyment. As we have done on many Christmases past, we celebrated every smile and every laugh that came from them. Through their amazed eyes and happy faces, we experienced Ireland all over again, but this time it was so much better, so much more memorable.

For me though, traveling and other such senior-life pursuits are just pleasant distractions. What comes after raising children is much more important to me.

Now I sit in the theater in our front row seats, permanently reserved for us, and watch our children take the stage. I have my date, my partner, my best friend, my lover, my wife, the mother of my children, at my side. We have our diet drinks, hers without ice. We hold our popcorn, buttered, of course, with additional salt sprinkled on the top. We sit back with our arms touching on the armrest. She squeezes my hand as the light dims. Our hearts are filled with pride as our children take the stage. In that second, from light to darkness, our hearts leap. In the darkness, my wife, whose face is softly lit by the stage lights, lifts a piece of popcorn to her mouth as she always does and I am awash with memory of the thrilling beginning of our journey to this theater. The curtains rise and so does our expectation. We read the opening credits with pride. We have produced and directed this play. We have tickets for life. It will be a show like no other.

One day we hope you will know the joy of children Even after they leave the nest, they continue to give you pride, joy and smiles. It is why Mom and I like to visit your performances. It is not because of a sense of obligation, but because how well you do was purchased by our loving and raising you. We have lifetime tickets to watch your performances, not just at venues and gigs, but at a endeavors throughout your life. Your success in life mirrors all of our love and care. We are your best fans. One day, perhaps, you will understand that your success and happiness are part of the reward that we as parents are given for nurturing you. We produced and directed this play.

CHAPTER THIRTEEN

See What We've Done

"One day, although we may be absent, we will be there, in the whisper of the wind and in the murmur from the trees."

Now, we visit the performances of Kevin's band, and we attend his monthly gig near Waikiki. We visit the shows of our son-in-law, Tyrone, and of Erin, and we enjoy music as we never did before. Now our lives are full of their successes, their songs, their good works, their music and their voices. We enjoy the adulation for them by their fans and friends, and we have become friends of their friends, and our circle of friends has widened and deepened. We have become the passive beneficiaries of their creativity and of the joy their creativity has brought to so many. When they are complimented, we are able to share in their satisfaction. Now, when they are not with us and we yearn to hear their voices or keep up to date on their activities, we click onto their websites or play their CDs.

We visit the new home, the university and the classroom where Kelly now lives and teaches as a professor. We eat in the cafeterias, marvel at the rose garden, rhododendrons, flowers, deep green lawns, fir trees and the beauty of the campus she works on, and we speak to her fellow faculty. Now she teaches and counsels her students -- the little strangers who had been taken in by parents like us and who grew into young adults. We attend her church services and meet her new friends and enjoy the camaraderie, the support and love of her church community. While we do all of this, we listen to the compliments, the admiration and the adulation heaped upon her. We are able to enjoy the pride of her successes and of ours through her. We enjoy the pride of loving her, the prettiest newborn the nurses in the OR had ever seen, now making a difference to the lives of many.

It is amazing when I look back on all those years. When those many years were the unforeseeable future, we started off as a couple in love and we became husband and wife. Now when that future has become the past, we see that together we made strangers into persons far, far better than we ever were. Through family we are empowered to make a difference beyond our mortal lives.

Even now when they are out of the house, they make our lives richer and fuller. When they travel to touch others with their songs, their talents, their hearts and their creativity and when they lift others with their friendship and kindness and their efforts, we are there. We are with them. When they shake a hand or embrace a soul, we are in that handshake and that embrace. One day, although we may be absent, we will be there, in the whisper of the wind and in the murmur from the trees. When they look into the mirror they will see us, and we will be in the eyes of their little strangers. When they look with love and pride into the eyes of their little strangers, we will be looking back at us.

Perhaps many of my thoughts seem inane and unimportant to some, even Pollyannaish. What I write of seems commonplace, even trite. What may be surprising though is that there is so much joy in these things that many of us take little notice of. Every moment of our lives is a gift. Because they do not come under a Christmas tree and are not wrapped in a ribbon, they go unnoticed. These moments are given to us to enjoy. Whether we enjoy them or not is up to us. It is not a wonder that what I say is true; the wonder is that we find it surprising.

I went to a birthday party for a pretty 2-year-old cousin. The party was held in a large room with a high vaulted ceiling and a smooth, lustrous cement floor. Around this community clubhouse were large, open and inviting spaces for play, and even a swimming pool that had been fenced and closed off.

Very soon this empty room began filling up with friends and relatives, some carrying gifts, packages and food, and toting many, many little children. People were hugging and kissing, shaking hands, exchanging tidings and remarking on how each had not changed and how good it was, after too long an absence, to see each other again. The older people sat down in chairs amidst the long tables lined in a row, watched the children and marveled at how big they'd grown. The younger adults visited with each other and strained to catch up with each other's past and present doings, and the children were bursting with the need to burn off enthusiasm in sight of the large, attractive open areas surrounding the building. Outside, children were dancing, jumping and marveling at a bubble machine that was filling the air with soapy globes. As fast as the bubbles were picked up by the breeze, the children were chasing them and popping them between their hands -- unless the bubbles were lucky enough to find their own way to a less violent death on the ground. A little girl raised her arms straight up over her head and did a war dance around the bubble machine while reciting a rhyme apparently learned and recited a hundred times in kindergarten. A little boy stood right by the bubble machine, raised his head in sync with the rising bubbles and screamed his delight. Other children were playing tag, hide-and-seek, and other games they made up. Still others were laughingly chasing each other around the large courtyard.

All these activities were observed smilingly by the parents as they talked and shared experiences with each other, with always one eye on their own children. "Stop that," said one. "Stay out of that area," yelled another. Off after her child rushed another. Inside, grandmothers carried infants and bounced them in their arms, hoping to be rewarded by smiles on little faces. It seemed that anything that would evince a smile was acceptable, even the most ridiculous facial expressions. One grandmother sat next to her granddaughter who was visiting from the mainland; she whispered into her ear solicitously to assuage her shyness and to coax her to join the games outside. Yet, another grandmother was singing softly to her toddler grandson whose feelings had been hurt. Another pulled on the string of a helium-filled balloon, moving it up and down to catch the fancy of the child her daughter held tightly to her bosom. A boy standing in the corner was trying to catch the eye of a pretty girl leaning up against the door. The air was filled with conversation, laughter and stories about children and grandchildren, about family and vacations, about each other and how fast their children were growing and time passing, about exhaustion from having to run after their "little bulldozers" and about how proud they were of them, about Johnny's difficulties at school and Malia's approaching return to the mainland after too short a stay with her grandparents.

The grandparents and great-grandparents surveyed the room contentedly, marveling at all of the life and activity that they had started, and in their wan and smiling faces, it was evident that they were satisfied with what they had done. This is now where Carol and I have come and now we will marvel at what we have done.

A little pretty two-year-old occasioned an event that brought together generations of families and scores of family friends and ignited an explosion of life. There it was in that clubhouse and the recreation center that day, all that we worked for, all that we strived for, the very meaning of our lives. Such events commonly occur, but are, for too many, commonplace, and maybe that is the source of many of our difficulties in life. We do not notice.

A good neighbor, who was moving to another state, asked me if they should sell their house. I advised that in all likelihood, over time, the value of the house would rise. They rented their house instead. Years later, after the value of their house had more than doubled, I received a long distance call from that former neighbor. She was disturbed because their rental house needed some minor repairs and the whole matter had been allowed to become an irritant to them. Addressing her distress over the irritant, I reminded her that while she rented her house it had more than doubled in value. I observed that: "It is as though you had discovered gold, but now you are complaining about having to dig it out of the ground." Seeing only the bad is a fault we too easily succumb to. Part of being content is to see the good, not to be blind to the bad, but to be focused on what is good, and as we strive for even more, to hold our ground and what we have.

It is the Christmas season, so it is time to take stock of the many gifts we have been given. Gifts are most often not wrapped with a nice ribbon and are not often placed under a tree. Because they aren't, we may never notice them. If we don't notice them, we can't really enjoy them. If we don't enjoy them, we cannot really be thankful for them.

Here is an example of how gifts come in small packages, but bring so much joy. Here is a remembrance that makes me smile just to think of it.

Mom and I accompanied Tyrone and Erin to a jewelry store. Erin wanted a wedding ring similar to the rings that I gave Mom for our engagement and wedding. The jeweler brought out displays of different rings for her to look at. When examining one of them, she said, "That diamond is too big." The jeweler, obviously caught off guard, said, "I never heard that one before." Hearing this, Tyrone stepped from the counter and while walking away not seeming to know I was in earshot, said under his breath, "I love that girl!"

That moment may have seemed insignificant to others, but its meaning was not lost on me. It is a gift you gave to me, and now I give it back to you. It is a gift that keeps giving. It is gift that makes me laugh. So, let us start noticing.

Gifts are here and there and everywhere. Most go unwrapped. To begin enjoying them, I guess, we should first notice them. A good place to start is to notice that we are alive. Life is a gift. Children and family are gifts. It is a miracle that you are breathing while reading this book. Now, it is up to you to take it from here.

To Our Children:

Here we are at the end of another year and it is time to assess all the things we are thankful for as we go forward. We must never let these times become dull habit. Each time is an opportunity to express to each other and to God our gratitude for what we have.

This, therefore, is your parents' Christmas 2003 message of thanks.

That we have had another year and that we are able to look forward to years ahead is itself a blessing.

We are thankful for our children, for our family, for our health and for our happiness and enjoyment of each other and of life. We are thankful that we can so freely express our love for each other; that we can and do smile, laugh and play together and that each moment shared is fresh, new and special.

We are thankful that PoPo and Kung Kung are still with us.

We are thankful that we can play together, look up at the ceiling while on our backs and laugh at stories and at each other; that we can joke, say and laugh at silly, unimportant little nothings just as we did when you were little children.

We are thankful that we can breathe out and breathe in and be filled with contentment; that we can laugh at a little yellow bird sticking its head out from under a shirt collar; that a dumb, lovable shaggy, and stinky dog can give us joy; that the cool sweet air wafting through a guava forest refreshes us in the morning as we awake to the chatter of tropical birds; that each other's arms are always open and each other's ears ready to listen; that we have such a large, supportive and loving extended family; that this wonderful circle of love is ever growing with the addition of Ella, Fischer, Hudson, Colton, Evan, Paige, Haley, Cambry, Cole, Ashton and so many, many more.

Happiness, in large part, is being truly thankful. Sincere gratitude derives from satisfaction and an appreciation for what one has already received. The key to happiness is knowing that we should be happy. We are happy for all we have, especially for you. You have made our lives rich and exciting. We are most thankful for you.

These words, all my emails and letters, my opinions and advice, I bequeath to my children. Although a lot of what I have said may be forgotten, these written words will not be. They are here, in this book in print, and more are kept in large white folders maintained in a room of our home. Long after I am gone, these words, like a friendly spirit, will follow my children and theirs. Eventually, my words will be replaced by their own, whispered lovingly into the ears of their own little strangers

Even if I am not around when my children have children, their children will know what their grandfather or great-grandfather said. They will know that -- but for the fact that I fell in love with the woman of my dreams and we took strangers into our home and loved them with all our might -- they may not be here today and may not be who they are. They will know that they too have posterity in their hands, and that it will be a grand and joyful mission only if they embrace it with love and take little strangers into their lives.

This is a father's love story. All stories begin and end. All things have a conclusion, and since it must be so, let this be the end of this writing and the beginning of your life with strangers. This was merely the sentiments of one father. If there is instruction here, it is that despite the myth that fathers are strong and do not cry, fathers do have feelings. We are able to love and we do. It is that from this father's point of view, falling in love with a good woman and raising little strangers is the greatest and most important occupation life offers. It is the greatest joy any man is privileged to have.

In a world where advertisements come in mailboxes, in pop-ups and spam, and on radio waves, in newspapers and magazines, and even now in theaters, we need to be reminded that there are things in life far, far more important and satisfying than luxury cars and designer clothes, fame and all that money can buy. There is the gift of a good woman and of loving strangers. It is life's gift, the gift of love. It is life.

My wish for all of you who read this is that there will be little strangers in your lives. When they come knocking, let them in, and fill the empty spaces in your home and in your hearts. The ability to bring strangers into the world, to invite them into our home and lives, to raise, nurture and love them, is a divine power to make a lasting contribution to charity, to posterity, to our church and our God, to those we love and to ourselves. To do so is an enduring prayer, a devotional that will continue beyond death. The truth is that we have children not for the sake of the children; the truth is that we have children for the sake of ourselves.

While we worked, loved, worried, fussed and fretted over our children, time has tip-toed past us without notice. We have grown old. I am left with images in my mind of all the time we have spent together as they were growing up. I am left with memories of the silly things they said and did, their funny laughter, their childish amazement, the feel of their trusting hands in mine, little arms that barely closed around my neck, cheeks pressing against mine, wondrous looks of puzzlement and of first impressions and the caress of unqualified love.

As my children move on, bitter and sweet, what remains is an album of memories to take with me on my final voyage. In the end, I must take my final trip without them. I am reminded of that mother bear growling fiercely, swatting at and chasing her cub away from her. Although I was horrified, I have come to understand, to accept, that it was her final act of love, bitter and sweet. The purest acts of love, it would seem, come on phantom feet on the wings of night, often mistaken and seldom noticed. It is all too, too bitter and sweet.

At night, in the darkness, I look to my left to assure that she is still sleeping comfortably by my side and in the quiet of our bedroom I listen for her breathing. My life now is to care for her, to make the quality of the rest of her life a reward for all she has done to make this story possible.

As for now.....well, my wife is making breakfast downstairs. The smell of bacon and eggs is having its effect. It is summoning me away from this computer. Those vittles are being prepared by the hands of my partner in this love story and so I will go downstairs to her.